GASTRO GEEK

Rejina Sabur-Cross

Photography by
Chris Terry

KYLE BOOKS LTD

First published in Great Britain in 2013 by
Kyle Books
23 Howland Street
London W1T 4AY
general.enquiries@kylebooks.com
www.kylebooks.com

10 9 8 7 6 5 4 3 2 1

ISBN 978-0-85783-106-4

Text © 2013 Rejina Sabur-Cross
Book design © 2013 Kyle Books Limited
Food photography © 2013 Chris Terry
Photostory photography © 2013 Joe Cross

Editor Emma Bastow
Editorial assistance Fiona Rose and Laura Foster
Design Nicky Collings and Aaron Blecha
Food photography Chris Terry
Styling Anna Jones
Copy editor Jane Bamforth
Production Gemma John and Nic Jones

A Cataloguing in Publication record for this title is available from the British Library.

Colour reproduction by ALTA London

Printed and bound in China by C&C Offset Ltd

CONTENTS

INTRODUCTION

Have a quick scan of the bookshelf you just plucked this from. Chances are it's saturated with beautifully bound tomes, brimming with misty-lensed shots of cakes and soft-focus loaves baked by celebrity hands in kitchens the size of your entire flat. There might be sections on salads, soups or desserts, but nothing to suggest what to rustle up when you're faced with little more than a can of chickpeas and some chopped tomatoes foraged from the back of the cupboard and less than half an hour to eat before you have to dash out again. Or what to cook when your boss is coming round for dinner, your flat looks like a pack of wolves have been at it and you're completely skint. And also quite possibly housebound, because the boiler repair guy still hasn't shown up. That's why I wanted to write this book. For people like us.

We want food that's exciting, cheap and dead clever. We want to dine on the different and the delicious. We want Mushy Pea Pakoras, Teriyaki Rice Burgers and Smoked Fish Sushi. We want to eat tasty, healthy grub for as little as possible, so we can focus on saving up for a week in the sun or that new frock. We want recipes for when we've come back after a late one, things to cook the morning after, and the night before, stuff to impress them with in the office and the kind of recipes that, like old friends, can be turned to again and again and won't let us down.

My culinary influences range from Dagenham to Dhakka and from Tottenham to Tokyo. A British-born Bengali, I've taught English in Japan and have also been massively influenced by the melting pot of cuisines on my East London doorstep. Nestled among the requisite canned beans and tomatoes in my kitchen cupboard you'll also spot miso paste, black lentils, tortillas, panko breadcrumbs and nigella seeds. Squirrelling these kinds of ingredients away is the key to producing exciting and flavoursome food at the drop of a hat.

Gastrogeek is a long overdue solution to everyday eating dilemmas. It's edgier than a supermodel's cheekbones, fresher than a very fresh thing and just a little bit rebellious. If you want to eat well without slipping into the red, and if you just want decent recipes that are genuine keepers, then this is my humble attempt to bridge that reality gap.

HARD UP AND
HUNGRY!

Let's face it. Everybody's skint. While it's all very well viewing celebrity chefs flitting betwixt Aga and wood-fired oven in their spotless kitchens, casually unwrapping brown paper packages of rare bred bovine, the reality is often very different. The reality is often you, with your clapped out Soviet era cooker, making do with that stringy brick of mince you fought over with a pensioner in the reduced aisle of your local supermarket. The magazines suggest you fritter the same amount on a frock as a weekend in Berlin and the rent's just gone up. Again.

Nonetheless, you cannot eat rubbish. Yes, you can have that wedge of artisan fromage from the fancy cheesemongers, but just a teensy bit, enough to crown the croutons on your apple and parsnip soup, instead of whopping great hunks of the stuff. This chapter is all about eating well without hitting the overdraft. It's about letting meat form the flavour foundation while allowing vegetables to take centre stage.

PROPER BEEF STOCK

Make this at least the day before you want to use it, allowing the flavours plenty of time to get hitched. Fill your sink with cold water and throw in a handful of salt. Leave the bones to soak for 10 minutes to draw out any blood.

Drain the water and place the bones in a large roasting dish with a few roughly hacked carrots, garlic cloves and onions, and a couple of bay leaves (if you're mega organised, freeze veg trimmings and scraps of meat and carcasses until you're ready to make the stock).

Sprinkle with a little oil and roast in the oven at 200°C/gas mark 6 for 40 minutes, until the bones are a good, dark chocolate colour. Tip the lot into a big pan, add some peppercorns, more salt and any herbs you like and cover with cold water.

Turn on the heat and simmer gently for 4-6 hours, skimming off any scum and making sure it never boils. Strain and leave to cool in the fridge overnight. The next day, lift off any fat that may have solidified and beneath you'll be rewarded with a deep mahogany liquid, loaded with fathoms of flavour.

FRENCH ONION SOUP

This takes a while but really the only 'work' once you've got it on the go is the odd stir every hour or so, because the hob puts in all the labour. An all-star cast consisting of decent stock, taking the onions to the very brink of caramelisation, but no further and of course that bubbling, molten cheese on toast topping.

Serves 6-8

For the soup
100g butter
2 tablespoons olive oil
1kg onions, sliced into thin crescents

1 bay leaf
salt
1 litre beef stock
1 Parmesan rind
½ tablespoon balsamic vinegar

Heat the butter and oil in a medium saucepan over the merest heat possible until the butter is melted. Add the onions, bay leaf and salt, stir well and cook for 1 hour. Continue to cook for another 1½ hours. Keep checking to make sure nothing is sticking or charred, until all the onions are completely caramelised and on the cusp of burning. Slosh in the beef stock, cheese heel and the balsamic vinegar and simmer for another hour.

To serve
1 baguette, sliced into rounds
1 clove garlic, halved

grated Gruyère or Emmental cheese
plenty of freshly ground black pepper
finely chopped fresh parsley

Preheat the grill to high and toast the baguette slices on one side. Rub with the garlic and sprinkle grated cheese on the untoasted side. Ladle the soup into heatproof serving bowls, top with the baguette and grill to golden perfection. Sprinkle with the black pepper and parsley.

GASTROGEEK

SZECHUAN BEEF CHEEK HOTPOT

Warming, rich, spicy and ever so slightly floral from the Szechuan peppercorns, there's very little actual effort involved (you can buy the peppercorns, rice wine and rock sugar online at www.wingyip.com, or from oriental supermarkets). Traditionally made with braising steak, I prefer the way in which beef cheeks yield at the merest suggestion of a spoon after aeons of slow, ponderous bubbling. It's beautiful the next day and even better the day after - it also freezes brilliantly, but I find it rarely makes it that far.

Serves 6-8

1 piece dried black fungus or 3 dried shiitake
    mushrooms (optional)
1kg beef cheeks, trimmed and diced
salt and freshly ground black pepper
1 teaspoon Szechuan peppercorns
1 cinnamon stick
3 star anise
1 tablespoon rice bran or sunflower oil
4 heaped teaspoons chilli bean paste
6 garlic cloves, finely chopped

3-4 spring onions, roughly chopped
45g fresh root ginger, peeled and finely
    chopped
plenty of turnips, leeks and sprouts, diced
50g yellow rock sugar or soft brown sugar
1 litre beef stock
2-3 tablespoons Shaoxing rice wine
1 tablespoon soy sauce
peel of 1 orange
plenty of greens and carrots, chopped
steamed brown rice, to serve

If using the dried mushrooms, set aside to soak, following the packet instructions.

Season the beef cheeks with salt and pepper and blanch them in boiling, salted water for a couple of minutes (this is to remove any scuzzy bits) then rinse and dice.

Toast the Szechuan peppercorns, cinnamon stick and star anise in a large, dry saucepan until fragrant. Set aside in a large bowl.

Add the oil to the pan and brown off the diced cheeks. A lot of juice will leach out - set this and the beef aside in the same bowl as the toasted spices, mixing well so the pan is left fairly dry, with just a little cooking liquid left.

Add the chilli bean paste, garlic, spring onions and ginger to the pan. Stir over a highish heat for a few moments. Once the garlic loses its raw edge and the chilli bean paste becomes fragrant, stir in the first batch of vegetables.

Tip in the spiced beef, soaked black fungus or mushrooms and soaking liquid (if using) and stir in the sugar, stock, rice wine, soy sauce and orange peel. Bring to the boil, cover and turn down to the lowest heat for 3 hours, stirring occasionally.

Towards the last 15 minutes of cooking time, add the carrots and greens and cook until tender. Dish up with plenty of steamed brown rice.

BORSCHT

with horseradish & dill cream

This deeply savoury, violently pink broth is brimming with hot, herbal goodness. It's given a Gillette of an edge with the horseradish and is super good for you to boot. The real deal is made with beef stock, but you can of course use vegetable.

Serves 6-8

For the horseradish and dill cream
1 tablespoon soured cream
2 teaspoons creamed horseradish
1 tablespoon chopped fresh dill
finely chopped beetroot tops
freshly ground black pepper
fresh dill, to garnish

In a small bowl, combine the soured cream, horseradish, dill, beetroot tops and black pepper. Set aside.

For the borscht
1 bunch beetroot (approximately 8), washed and tops set aside
few sprigs of thyme
4 garlic cloves, unpeeled
2 teaspoon salt
2 tablespoons olive oil
2 onions, diced
¼ cabbage, shredded
1 carrot, diced
2 tablespoons vodka
1 teaspoon sugar
1 litre beef stock
1 bay leaf

Preheat the oven to 150°C/gas mark 2. Wrap the beetroot in foil with the thyme, whole garlic cloves, 1 teapoon of salt and half the olive oil. Bake for 30–40 minutes or until tender. Cool, peel and roughly chop the garlic and beetroot.

Heat the remaining oil in a saucepan and when it's hot add the onion, cabbage and carrot, vodka, sugar and remaining salt. Tip in the roasted garlic and beetroot. Sweat briefly and then pour in the beef stock and add the bay leaf. Simmer for 15–20 minutes.

Liquidise the soup in batches until smooth and return to the pan. To serve, gently reheat, ladle into hot soup bowls and serve with a generous dollop of the horseradish and dill cream and a light shower of dill.

CRISPY PEKING MUTTON BREAST

If you're a craver of Chinese crispy duck then you'll go ruddy mental for this. Yes, it takes a couple of days plus a couple of cooking methods, but it's actually just a case of sticking everything in a saucepan and leaving it all to putter away followed by a swift torching under a hot grill plus a spot of sauce reduction the next day. Like all the best dishes, the results are more than worth the wait. Crunchy, fatty, salty – diet food this most certainly is not. You can get a whole mutton breast with generous change from a fiver. Yet more proof that you don't need to spend a fortune to eat really, really well.

Serves 2

For the mutton breast
800g–1kg unrolled mutton breast or
    lamb breast
100ml dark soy sauce
1 tablespoon chilli bean sauce
4cm piece fresh root ginger, peeled
    and grated
3 cinnamon sticks
30g yellow rock sugar or brown sugar

4 star anise
6 dried Chinese mushrooms or
    shiitake mushrooms or 1 large piece
    of dried black fungus
1 tablespoon clear honey
2 tablespoons Shaoxing rice wine
4 garlic cloves, grated or crushed
3 spring onions, roughly chopped
1 teaspoon salt, plus extra for sprinkling
2 litres lamb stock

The day before you want to eat, lob all the ingredients for the mutton into a large saucepan, the lamb should be submerged in the stock. Simmer for 4 hours with the lid on. Chuck away your scented candles – your kitchen will smell fantastic!

Remove the lamb and place in a large bowl. Cover with clingfilm. Strain the remaining fatty liquid into another bowl, cover with clingfilm and chill both bowls in the fridge overnight.

The next day, remove the bowls from the fridge. Lift the layer of solid fat from the liquid bowl and discard. Pour the liquid into a pan and heat to reduce until thick and treacly.

Preheat the grill to high. Shred the lamb and sprinkle it liberally with salt. Place under a hot grill until crisp.

To serve
lettuce leaves or Chinese pancakes
    (from major supermarkets)

plum sauce
cucumber and spring onion strips

Heat the pancakes according to the packet instructions. Serve the lamb, plum sauce, spring onions, cucumber strips and the reduced sauce, wrapped in leaves of 1 medium iceberg lettuce or warm pancakes.

CURRIED BONE MARROW ON TOAST

with blood orange, chilli and coriander salad

I was so happy when I first heard this salad was served at St. John in London. For years I had thought it was just my crazy mother that was into bone marrow. She used to cook up the most wonderful bone-in lamb curries, and my brother and I would fight over the prized spicy butter of marrow with primal and hedonistic abandon. Here I've created my own curried version of Fergus Henderson's English classic, by roasting it with curry salt and serving with a Bengali-style salad. If you're making a lamb curry ask the butcher for bits of bone with marrow in, it really does make all the difference.

Serves 2

1 teaspoon salt
½ teaspoon curry powder
1 garlic clove, crushed
6 x 10cm pieces of lamb bone marrow
1 small bunch fresh coriander,
   finely chopped
¼ red onion, very finely sliced

1 blood orange, peeled and segmented
juice of ½ lemon
½ teaspoon salt
2 tablespoons olive oil
1 or 2 fresh green chillies, finely chopped
   (deseeded if you're a coward like me)
4 slices of your favourite bread, toasted
freshly ground black pepper

Preheat the oven to 190°C/gas mark 5.

Make a curry salt by mixing the salt and curry powder together, then mash the crushed garlic into this to create a paste.

Smear this over either end of the bone marrow pieces, making sure you cover the end bits where the marrow is exposed. Roast for about 15-20 minutes (you don't want to leave it in there for too long or it will disintegrate). The marrow should be loose, melting and quite crisp at the ends.

Place the coriander, red onion and blood orange in a bowl. Dress with lemon juice, salt, olive oil and chopped green chilli, toss gently to combine.

Pop the bread in the toaster and when it is ready cut off the crusts. Spread the hot toast with the marrow (scoop it out with a teaspoon handle), season with pepper and top with the salad.

ROAST TOMATO PUTTANESCA

wow!

Roasting tomatoes adds an entirely new dimension to this bolshy, in-your-face dirty stopout of pasta sauces. It pretty much blows those jarred sauces out of the pasta water. The vinegared piquancy of marinated anchovies (from the deli section at the supermarket) adds a pleasing tang, but you can always use the canned salted variety if you're not a fan. An absolute keeper, it's one to turn to time and again.

Serves 2

9 medium vine tomatoes
pinch of sugar
salt and freshly ground black pepper
2 tablespoons chilli oil or olive oil
3 garlic cloves (2 grated or crushed,
   1 thinly sliced)
12 marinated anchovies
½ teaspoon dried chilli flakes

a good glug of red wine
1 Parmesan rind
225g dried spaghetti
8 fat green pitted olives, chopped
1 tablespoon capers in brine, drained
   and chopped
1-2 tablespoons chopped fresh parsley,
   to garnish
grated Parmesan cheese, to serve

Preheat the oven to 150°C/gas mark 2. Halve the tomatoes and place cut side up in a roasting tin. Sprinkle with the sugar and season with salt and pepper. Roast for about 1 hour or until singed in places and well roasted.

Gently warm the chilli or olive oil in a medium pan. Add all the garlic and heat gently without colouring for about 10 minutes.

Add the marinated anchovies and dried chilli and stir until the anchovies disintegrate.

Turn up the heat, add the red wine, the roasted tomatoes and Parmesan rind and simmer over a low-medium heat for about 20 minutes.

Cook the spaghetti according to the packet instructions. Drain the pasta. Then immediately stir the olives and capers into the sauce and toss well with the drained spaghetti. Garnish with parsley, sprinkle over the grated Parmesan and serve.

SMOKED MACKEREL MAKI
with wasabi mayonnaise

This is a classic example of how it's possible to eat tasty, healthy treats on the cheap. Go for the best smoked mackerel you can afford and try to get it from a fishmonger. However, don't stress too much if you can only get hold of high street stuff. Decent sushi rice, rice vinegar, nori sheets; these things are not cheap either, but it's all relative. If you compare how much you'd spend on the same amount of ready-made sushi, and how many portions you'll be able to make, you really are doing your bank balance a favour.

Serves 4-6

For the rice
300g sushi rice, washed, and drained for about 30 minutes

1 small piece dried seaweed
4 tablespoons rice vinegar
1 teaspoon soy sauce
2 tablespoons caster sugar

Tip the rice into a saucepan and add 330ml cold water. Add the seaweed, cover with a lid and bring to the boil over a medium heat. Simmer for about 5-7 minutes, before turning the heat off and leaving it to steam, still covered for 10-15 minutes. The rice should be perfectly cooked through and all the water absorbed. Set aside to cool.

Stir the rice vinegar, soy sauce and sugar together until the sugar dissolves. Once the rice has cooled down a little, fold the vinegar mixture in and combine gently but well.

For the wasabi mayonnaise
1 tablespoon mayonnaise

½-1 tablespoon wasabi paste
1 teaspoon soy sauce

Mix the ingredients together, adjusting the amount of wasabi according to taste and set aside.

For the filling
1 x packet of 10 toasted nori sheets
1 smoked mackerel, skinned, flaked and picked over for bones

½ medium cucumber, cut into strips
4 spring onions, cut into strips
2 avocados, in strips, sprinkled with lemon juice

Place a nori sheet, glossy side down, on a bamboo sushi mat. Spread enough rice to form a thin layer all over, leaving a 3cm margin around three of the edges and a slightly thicker margin at the furthest end away from you.

Layer a line of fish, cucumber, avocado and spring onion strips along the margin of rice closest to you. Smear a blob of the wasabi mayonnaise across this and brush the uncovered nori furthest away from you with water.

Carefully roll up the sushi, sealing the open end of seaweed by pressing down gently where you have brushed the seaweed with water, and roll gently back and forth until the whole thing feels like it's securely sealed. Unroll the mat and wet the blade of a long, sharp knife under cold running water. Slice the roll carefully into bite-size pieces. Eat while the rice is still warmish.

PRAWN & LEEK CROQUETTES

Some people like to fritter away their hard earned dosh on fancy moisturisers; others like to spend their money down the pub. For me, it's prawn croquettes. A good, rich béchamel sauce, enriched with prawn, paprika and a delicate crisp, Gouda-flecked panko shell. I like to make these after one of those days. You know the one when the train got cancelled and the sadistic white van driver decided to aim for the enormous puddle just in front of you. I use sustainably caught prawns. Biting into one of these beauties always tints everything a fetching shade of rose.

Serves 4-6

1 medium onion
6 cloves
400ml whole milk
1 bay leaf
2 tablespoons olive oil
60g butter
1 clove garlic, crushed
1 leek or 1 onion, finely diced
60g plain flour
220g peeled prawns

2-3 tablespoons shredded spring greens
salt and freshly ground black pepper
¼ teaspoon freshly grated nutmeg
½ teaspoon smoked paprika
2 eggs, beaten
50g Gouda cheese, grated
150g panko breadcrumbs
groundnut oil, for frying
flour, for shaping
lemon wedges, to serve

Stud the onion with the cloves and place in a small pan, add the milk and bay leaf and warm very gently over a low heat.

Heat the oil and butter in a medium pan and fry the garlic and leek or onion for 5 minutes, until soft and just beginning to brown. Turn the heat down to low and stir in the flour, cook for about 10 minutes.

Add the prawns and greens and continue to cook until the prawns have just turned from pink to grey (a minute or two) and the greens have wilted a little.

Strain the warmed milk and slowly add it to the prawn mixture, stirring constantly until the sauce is the texture of a slightly runny mash. Season with salt, pepper, nutmeg and paprika. Leave to cool and cover with clingfilm. Refrigerate for a couple of hours or overnight if possible.

When you're ready for action, have the beaten eggs in one bowl and the cheese and panko mixed together in another.

Heat the oil to 180°C (or drop in a cube of stale bread, it should take 1 minute to brown) and line a plate with kitchen paper. With floury hands, roll tablespoonfuls of the chilled mixture into 16 cylinders, dip in the egg and then the crumbs.

Deep fry in batches of 3 for 3-4 minutes, until golden, remove from the oil with a slotted spoon and drain on kitchen paper. Serve at once with lemon wedges and a glass of sherry.

PEA, PARSLEY & MATURE CHEDDAR DIP

with pumpkin seed crackers

This is one of my all time favourite dips, and the crackers are insanely easy to make – in fact every time I'm in the supermarket and I see those expensive packets of gourmet crackers, I always remember just what a piece of cake it is to bake these and make a beeline straight for the flour section instead. Spelt and rye can add up, so if you're feeling the pinch go for wholemeal and plain or whatever you can afford. Perfect for snacking on in front of the telly or passing round with drinks.

Serves 4

For the dip
1 garlic clove
1 teaspoon salt
150g frozen petits pois, defrosted
2 tablespoons soured cream
2 tablespoons mayonnaise
1-2 tablespoons finely chopped fresh parsley
70g mature Cheddar cheese, grated
25g toasted pine nuts
1 tablespoon chives, finely chopped
1 teaspoon garlic powder
freshly ground black pepper

Crush the garlic clove with 1 teaspoon of salt to form a paste. Transfer to a bowl and add the remaining dip ingredients. Blitz together using a hand-held electric blender and place in the fridge to chill.

For the crackers
50g plain or spelt flour, plus extra for dusting
50g wholemeal or rye flour
5 teaspoons of seeds of your choice
3 tablespoons grated Parmesan
  or other hard cheese, for sprinkling
pinch of salt

In a bowl, mix the flours with about 6 tablespoons of water to form a supple dough. Turn a roasting tin or baking sheet upside down, dust it with flour and roll the dough out to cover the tin. It should be nice and thin, don't worry if it doesn't look perfect.

Preheat the oven to 180°C/gas mark 4. Sprinkle the dough with a little water and from a slight height (to ensure even distribution) sprinkle over the seeds, cheese and a pinch of salt. Pop the inverted tin in the oven and bake for 15-20 minutes or until golden and crisp.

Remove and slide a spatula under to loosen the cracker before breaking up into big bite-size shards.

Serve the hot crackers with the cold dip. Any leftover crackers will keep in an airtight container for a few days.

KALE & CANNELLINI BEAN SOUP

with cider and smoked Cheddar rye bread

Bursting with massive, baritone flavours, despite being unbelievably easy on the purse, this soup has got it all. Make this on a rainy Sunday and you can come home to a hearty bowl of nourishing goodness the next day. The soup freezes well so it can be made in batches and defrosted when you want to eat it. If you want to be uber flash, you can split the bread dough into four, make individual loaves and then hollow these out before filling with the soup, sprinkling with the cheese and grilling to melty perfection.

Serves 4

For the bread
450g rye flour
180ml dry cider
1 teaspoon cider vinegar

1 teaspoon active dried yeast
70g smoked Cheddar cheese, diced
1-2 tablespoons chopped fresh sage leaves
    (stems reserved)
1½ teaspoons salt

Place 150g of the rye flour, the cider, cider vinegar and yeast in a bowl, stir well, cover and leave to ferment for 6 hours.

Stir the smoked cheese, sage leaves, 150ml warm water, salt and the remaining 300g of rye flour into the bread mix. Leave for 30 minutes. Pat the bread into a roundish ball and place on some baking parchment. Slash a few gashes over the top and lower into a 9cm ovenproof pot. Leave for 2 hours to rise somewhere nice and warm.

After 2 hours pop a lid on the bread pot. Place the bread in an unheated oven and turn to 200°C/gas mark 6. Bake the bread for 30 minutes, remove the lid from the bread pot and bake for another 15 minutes until cooked all the way through and hollow when tapped. Serve hot with the soup.

For the soup
1 tablespoon olive oil
1 onion, diced
2 garlic cloves, finely chopped
2 medium carrots, diced
2 small leeks, finely chopped
2 sticks celery, finely chopped
1 sausage, sliced thinly

100g dried cannellini beans, soaked overnight
    in cold water
½ teaspoon dried thyme
1 bay leaf
1 glass red wine or 2 tablespoons
    sherry vinegar
1½ litres chicken stock
1 Parmesan rind
100g kale, finely shredded

In a large saucepan, heat the olive oil and fry the onion, garlic, carrots, leeks, celery and sausage. Drain the soaked beans and add them to the pan with the thyme, reserved sage stems and bay leaf. Turn the heat up and tip in the wine or sherry vinegar. Once that's reduced add the stock and the Parmesan rind, reduce the heat and leave to simmer for a couple of hours. Cook for a further 45 minutes whilst the bread is baking. Add the kale to the simmering soup for the last 15 minutes of the cooking time.

CAULIFLOWER VICHYSSOISE

with cauliflower cheese crisps

Who said that you can't eat elegant, swanky food when you're hard up? This is a properly sophisticated potage to be delicately supped in the more summery months. The flavours of the cauliflower are stunningly accented when served chilled in a way that just doesn't register when eaten hot. Simply spiffing enjoyed outdoors with a crisp, cold glass of white wine.

Serves 4

1 cauliflower, leaves removed and cut into florets
olive oil, for sprinkling
1 teaspoon salt, plus extra for sprinkling
1 teaspoon cumin seeds

500ml whole milk
1 onion, quartered
1 bay leaf
140g smoked Cheddar cheese, grated
freshly ground black pepper
2 tablespoons finely snipped fresh chives

Preheat the oven to 170°C/gas mark 3. Take a couple of cauliflower florets and slice them very thinly. Lay these on a baking sheet and drizzle with a little olive oil and a little salt. Roast the cauliflower slices for 5–8 minutes on each side, until golden. Turn the oven off and set the cauliflower slices aside.

Toast the cumin seeds in a hot, non-stick, dry frying pan until fragrant. Grind the toasted seeds to a powder, using a pestle and mortar.

Very gently heat the milk, onion, bay leaf and remaining cauliflower florets together in a saucepan for 30–45 minutes until tender.

Remove the onion and bay leaf and add 120g of the grated cheese. Stir until melted and add the ground roasted cumin and salt. Blitz with a hand-held electric blender until smooth. Set aside to cool.

Turn the oven back on to 170°C/gas mark 3. Place the roasted cauliflower slices on baking parchment. Shape the remaining grated cheese into rounds over the roasted cauliflower slices and return to the oven for 8–10 minutes or until they've formed lightly tanned discs (be careful they don't go too brown or they'll taste acrid). Allow to cool.

Cover and chill the soup thoroughly, sprinkle with black pepper and chives and serve with the cauliflower cheese crisps.

SMOKED AUBERGINE STUFFED PARATHAS
with cumin steam-fried potatoes

The paratha rolling and folding can seem a bit faffy, but once you've had that first scoop of gently spiced spud with flaky, buttery paratha leaves, you'll want to put in the extra rolling-pin time. And you can always make the dough the night before and keep it airtight in the fridge. The potatoes are very thinly sliced and steam-fried until tender but crisp and the judicious spicing means the flavour of the vegetable rules.

Makes 3

For the smoked aubergine filling
1 medium aubergine
1 teaspoon nigella seeds

1 shallot, finely chopped or ½ red onion, finely chopped
1 tablespoon finely chopped fresh coriander
½ teaspoon salt

Flame-roast the aubergine over a gas hob on a low heat, until blackened all over. (Alternatively, roast in the oven at 220°C/gas mark 7 for 20-25 minutes.) Peel the aubergine and mash the creamy innards with the remaining ingredients.

For the parathas
200g wholewheat chapati flour
150g plain flour

1 teaspoon salt
3 tablespoons olive oil, plus extra for frying
25g butter

Mix the flours and salt. Make a well and gradually add the oil and enough cold water to form a soft, pliable dough. Divide the dough into 6 equal pieces. Melt the butter in a frying pan. Roll out a piece of dough to the size of a dinner plate. Smear a teaspoon of melted butter in the centre, fold in half, and then in half again, then roll out again to the same size plate. Repeat 2-3 times. Repeat with the remaining dough, layering the dough circles with foil to separate them.

Take one of the dough circles and spoon over one-third of the aubergine mix. Carefully drape a second circle of dough over the aubergine smeared one. Gently seal the edges, being careful not to let any filling ooze out! Repeat to make 2 more parathas.

To cook the parathas, reheat the frying pan and add 1 tablespoon olive oil. When it's really sizzling hot, carefully slide in 1 stuffed paratha and fry for 10-15 minutes, until golden, puffy and blistered on both sides with brown spots. Repeat to cook the remaining parathas.

For the cumin potatoes
25g butter
1 tablespoon olive oil
2-3 medium potatoes, peeled and sliced into matchsticks

1 teaspoon cumin seeds, toasted and ground
pinch of salt
tomato ketchup and chilli sauce, to serve

Heat the butter and olive oil in the pan and gently sauté the potatoes for about 5 minutes. Add the cumin and salt and cover with a lid to steam for 10-15 minutes. Turn the heat to low and cook until tender. Remove the lid and turn the heat up to crisp the chips. Serve them rolled up in the paratha with a big dollop of chilli sauce mixed with tomato ketchup.

HOUSE-BOUND!

We've all been there haven't we? 6pm and still skulking around the flat in our jim jams, without the remotest inclination to go anywhere near the big, bad outside world. Ill, hung over, snowed in or waiting for the boiler repairman, we've all had days when we just can't be bothered to go out and make like a hunter gatherer. This is when the nerve centre of the home, a well stocked kitchen cupboard, swings into action. It really doesn't have to be all orange gloop on toast, if you squirrel away a tin of chilli beans here and a packet of tortillas there, every time you do make it to the electronic self service area, you should find yourself with all manner of wondrous things to chow next time you raid the larder. With a bit of imagination, you need never again answer the door to exchange far too much of your hard earned dosh for a soggy box of disappointment from an underpaid man in a motorbike helmet. Whether it's a speedy spinach, egg, coconut and tamarind curry or the fruitiest, fat rascals scarfed hot from the oven, there are a surprising number of options once you really put your mind to it. These can be as indulgent or as virtuous as you like. It's a good idea to ensure there are enough ingredients hanging about for at least four or five of the following recipes to be readily available on standby at any given moment.

SPRING GREEN & STILTON SPELT-OTTO

One of those grains that's likely to find itself shoved away at the back of the cupboard is spelt. There behind the more popular pasta quills and the rice, it's lovely, nubbly nuttiness missing from so many a kitchen cupboard supper. By using it instead of Arborio in a risotto you get a real textural treat, here it positively erupts with creamy, salted zesty tang. Deeply comforting and easy to throw together, you can always substitute the chicken stock for vegetable if you're feeding the meat-averse. The pairing of cabbage and Stilton here is absolutely king.

Serves 4

250g spelt
30g butter
1 tablespoon olive oil
1 onion, finely chopped
2 garlic cloves, finely chopped
1 celery stick, diced
1 tablespoon chopped fresh rosemary leaves
150ml white wine
600ml hot vegetable stock

50g Parmesan cheese, grated
1 tablespoon double cream
squeeze of lemon juice
250g spring cabbage, greens or spinach, finely chopped
150g Stilton, Gorgonzola or dolcelatte cheese (or any other blue cheese)
25g pine nuts, toasted
freshly ground black pepper

Soak the spelt in cold water for 10 minutes. Drain.

Heat the butter and oil in a large frying pan and fry the onion, garlic and celery over a low heat, for about 10 minutes, without colouring.

Add the drained spelt and rosemary. Turn the heat up, slosh in the wine and reduce.

Gradually add the hot stock, stirring until the spelt is cooked through – about 45 minutes.

Add the Parmesan, cream and lemon juice and stir through. Add the greens and cook until they've just lost their rawness – about 3 minutes.

Crumble in the Stilton until it just begins to melt but still has a few whole chunks. Serve with toasted pine nuts sprinkled over the top and lots of black pepper.

CHEESE & HERB SCONES

with garlic & chive cream

This is my cunning savoury take on the traditional cream tea. An excellent way of using up any odds and sods of old cheese you might have lurking around in the back of the fridge. They'll keep in an airtight container for a few days but are at their prime served straight from the oven with a nice pot of Lady Grey.

Makes 10-12

For the scones
vegetable oil, for greasing
500g plain flour, plus extra for dusting
3 teaspoons baking powder
2 teaspoons fresh thyme leaves
½ teaspoon cayenne pepper
pinch of smoked paprika
2 spring onions, finely chopped

250g Cheddar or Red Leicester cheese
  (or any other hard cheese), grated
salt and freshly ground black pepper
1 egg
250ml whole milk, plus extra for brushing
1 teaspoon truffle oil
2 teaspoons olive oil
milk and grated cheese, for topping

Preheat the oven to 220°C/gas mark 7. Brush a baking tray generously with oil.

In a large mixing bowl, combine the flour, baking powder, thyme, cayenne, paprika, spring onions, 225g of the grated cheese, 1 teaspoon of salt and plenty of black pepper. Mix the egg, milk and oils in a jug and slowly trickle into the dry ingredients. Stir well until a soft dough is formed.

Dust a work surface with flour and roll the dough out to just over 2.5cm thick (make sure you don't roll it too thinly). To create a natural 'split' in the scone, fold the dough in half, back over itself and lightly roll out again. Using a 6cm cutter (or an inverted glass) cut out round shapes. There's a theory that if you can do this in one clean cut, without having to twist the cutter or glass too much you'll be rewarded with a better rise. Place on the oiled baking tray and brush with milk. Sprinkle with the remaining grated cheese.

For the garlic and chive cream
1 garlic bulb, sliced in half horizontally
olive oil, for drizzling
salt

handful of snipped fresh chives
250ml soured cream
tomato relish, red onion marmalade or pickle,
  to serve

Put the garlic halves on a small square of foil, drizzle with the oil and sprinkle with salt. Wrap up into a loose parcel. Bake the scones and garlic parcel for about 20 minutes or until the scones are well risen and golden and the garlic tender. Put the scones on a wire rack to cool slightly.

Squeeze the roast garlic out of the skin and mash it to a pulp. Mix the garlic with the chives and stir into the soured cream. Split and smother the scones with the cream. Serve immediately with tomato relish, red onion marmalade or pickle.

CHICKPEA & TOMATO CURRY

spicy!

A nifty little cuzza to have up your sleeve, this ticks every box – brimming with flavour, its stupendously healthy and if you've already got most of the spices, costs very, very little to make. You basically just need a can of tomatoes, a can of chickpeas and a bit of a spice raid. Serve with rice, flatbreads, lashings of cucumber raita and salad.

Serves 2

2 tablespoons olive oil
1 teaspoon mustard seeds
1 teaspoon cumin seeds
1 small onion, chopped
160g potato, peeled and diced
20g fresh root ginger, peeled and grated
3 garlic cloves, crushed
½ teaspoon turmeric

½ teaspoon chilli powder
1 heaped teaspoon curry powder
2 teaspoons salt
1 fresh green chilli, quartered
400g can chickpeas, drained
400g can chopped tomatoes
1 teaspoon sugar
juice of ½ lemon
1-2 tablespoons fresh coriander leaves

Heat the olive oil in a saucepan. Once it's hot add the mustard and cumin seeds.

As soon as they start to crackle, add the onion, potato, ginger, garlic, turmeric, chilli powder, curry powder, 1 teaspoon salt, green chilli and 100ml water.

Give it all a good stir and cover. Leave to cook over a low heat until the potatoes are tender, adding more water if necessary. Add the drained chickpeas and chopped tomatoes and cook for a further 5 minutes over a low heat.

Finally add another teaspoon of salt, the sugar and lemon juice and simmer for 15 minutes. Strew with the coriander, simmer for a further 15 minutes and serve.

DUCK EGG, SPINACH & COCONUT CURRY

Duck eggs take to robust spices in much the same way their creators do to water. You can of course, use standard hen's eggs if you don't have any duck ones to hand. Known as dimer jhol in Bengali, this was a regular midweek tea when I was growing up. Creamed coconut injects a sublime silkiness while the tamarind and lime chutney add sufficient mouth-pop to make this a store cupboard favourite you'll fall back on again and again.

Serves 4

2 duck eggs, or 3 hen's eggs
5 green cardamom pods
2 teaspoons coriander seeds
1 teaspoon fenugreek leaves
1 teaspoon cumin seeds
1 tablespoon olive oil
1 teaspoon mustard seeds
6 curry leaves
1 large onion, diced
1 tablespoon chopped fresh root ginger

3 garlic cloves, crushed
2 green chillies
75g yellow split lentils
½ teaspoon turmeric
75g creamed coconut, grated
1 teaspoon tamarind pulp
600ml chicken or vegetable stock
2 teaspoons lime chutney
salt and sugar, to season
zest and juice of 1 lime
100g spinach

Place the duck eggs in a pan of cold water, bring to the boil and simmer for 10 minutes. Cool under running cold water, peel and halve.

Toast the cardamom pods, coriander, fenugreek and cumin seeds in a hot, non-stick, dry frying pan until fragrant. Tip into a spice mill or pestle and mortar and grind roughly.

Heat the olive oil in a saucepan and once it's hot, add the mustard seeds. Once they start to pop add the curry leaves, onion, ginger, garlic and chillies, along with the ground toasted spices.

Add the lentils and turmeric and stir for a minute or two. Add the coconut, tamarind, stock and chutney and cook over a low heat until the lentils are tender (around 30–40 minutes).

Finally, stir in a good pinch of salt and sugar. Season with the lime zest and juice, fold in the spinach leaves and add the duck eggs.

STEAMED & SMOKED LAPSANG SOUCHONG CHICKEN

I've got a real thing about smoked stuff. I don't know if this has something to do with being an ex-Golden Virginia girl, but anything with that woody burnt top note – be it fish, chicken, vegetable or salt really does it for me. Smoking (food) in your own kitchen is surprisingly easy. Steaming the chicken first helps to lock in moisture, otherwise things can end up a bit arid. The flavour is quite subtle, so I like to use a heavily perfumed leaf like lapsang souchong, but any decent loose tea will do. Oh, and don't forget to stick the batteries back in the smoke alarm afterwards...

Serves 4

2 garlic cloves, crushed
3cm piece fresh root ginger, peeled (reserve the peel) and grated
1 teaspoon Shaoxing rice wine
1 teaspoon sesame oil
2 chicken legs
1 teaspoon clear honey, plus extra for brushing

1 teaspoon soy sauce, plus extra for brushing
2 star anise
peel of 1 satsuma or clementine
100g rice
100g dark brown sugar
25g Lapsang Souchong tea leaves
rice and pak choy, to serve

Start by mixing the garlic, ginger, rice wine and sesame oil together. Push your fingers between the skin and flesh of the chicken and feed this mixture in through the gaps you've created. Brush the chicken with the honey and soy sauce and place in a bamboo steamer.

Bring about 2.5cm water to boil in a wok, over a high heat and add the star anise plus the satsuma or clementine and ginger peels.

Place the bamboo steamer of chicken in the wok and seal tightly with foil and a heavy lid. Steam for about 30 minutes. Remove the steamer from the wok, pour out the liquid and line the base with three layers of foil.

Mix together the rice, sugar and tea leaves and sprinkle it over the foil. Place the steamer on top and brush the chicken legs with soy sauce and honey. Cover the lot tightly with foil ensuring everything's as airtight as possible. Place over a lowish heat and smoke for 30 minutes.

Preheat the oven to 220°C/gas mark 7. Finally, roast the chicken in the oven for about 10 minutes, to get the skin super crisp. Serve with rice and steamed pak choy.

MUSHY PEA PAKORAS

with chilli beetroot raita

A real old-fashioned chip-shop treat 'oop north' is the mushy pea fritter. I adore the gentle sweetness and texture of mushy peas. They're especially good whipped up in a pakora, for a harmonious combo of spiced crunch and fluffy interior. Mushy peas are quite wet, so you will need to add a fair bit of rice flour. Blooming gorgeous with lashings of chilli beetroot raita and a steaming mug of builder's.

Serves 4

For the raita
4 tablespoons Greek yogurt

1 cooked beetroot, grated
1 teaspoon chilli sauce
2 tablespoons chopped fresh mint

Combine the raita ingredients and chill.

For the pakoras
300g can mushy peas
2 tablespoons fresh mint leaves, finely chopped
2 garlic cloves, crushed
½ teaspoon turmeric
1 teaspoon cumin seeds
1 fresh green chilli, finely chopped

½ teaspoon chilli powder
½ teaspoon sugar
1 teaspoon curry powder
½ teaspoon salt
1 onion, finely chopped
40g rice flour
40g chickpea (gram) flour
vegetable oil, for deep frying

Tip the peas into a mixing bowl and stir in the mint. Add the garlic, turmeric, cumin, fresh chilli, chilli powder, sugar, curry powder and salt, stir well. Add the onions and flour and mix well for about 2–3 minutes until the mixture is fairly thick and dry.

Heat the oil in a wok or saucepan until hot enough to deep fry, (about 190°C or drop in a cube of stale bread, it should take 40 seconds to brown) then drop in 4 tablespoons of the mixture at a time. You can make quenelles using a couple of spoons to shape the mixture into ovals, if you want them to look consistent. Cook for 6–8 minutes, or until golden and crisp. Drain on kitchen paper and serve immediately with the raita and a cuppa.

SLAVIC STUFFED CABBAGE LEAVES

A blinding way to make a little meat go the distance. This is comfort food brought to you by the people who know hearty, wholesome, peasant grub better than anyone else. East European-style, tender stuffed cabbage leaves smothered with a creamy, tomato sauce. For a full on Slavic feast serve with Borscht (page 13) and vodka shots.

Serves 4-6

1 savoy cabbage, trimmed and separated into leaves
2 tablespoons olive oil
1 onion, diced
3 cloves garlic, finely chopped
2 carrots, finely diced
½ large leek, finely chopped
1 parsnip, finely diced
250g chestnut or closed cup mushrooms
1 bay leaf
1–2 teaspoons Worcestershire sauce
115g long grain rice
750ml lamb stock

500g minced lamb
100g mixed nuts, chopped roughly
1–2 tablespoons mixed chopped fresh herbs e.g. sage parsley and thyme
salt and freshly ground black pepper
½ teaspoon smoked paprika
1 large glass red wine
2 tablespoons tomato purée
1 teaspoon Dijon mustard
1 tablespoon plain flour
250ml crème fraîche,
1 tablespoon chopped fresh chives or dill
crème fraîche and dill, to serve

Bring a large pan of salted water to boil. Add a few cabbage leaves at a time and blanch for 30 seconds. Remove, rinse under cold water, squeeze to remove any excess water, leaving just damp enough to stick together when rolled up.

Heat 1 tablespoon of the olive oil in a large, deep frying pan. Fry the onion, garlic, carrot, leek, parsnip and mushrooms with the bay leaf and Worcestershire sauce until everything is brown and caramelised. Stir in the rice and 250ml of stock. Simmer until the rice is cooked and all the liquid has been absorbed. In a large mixing bowl, combine the mince, nuts, mixed herbs, salt, pepper and smoked paprika. Stir the cooked vegetables and rice into the mince mixture.

Cut the larger cabbage leaves in half (removing any woody stems) and place a spoonful of the mixture in the centre of each half. Roll this up in the same way you would a burrito, wetting the edges of the leaf, rolling up the centre and tucking the corners of the leaf into itself at the end. Using the same frying pan, heat the remaining oil and brown the cabbage rolls. Turn the heat up and pour the wine all around the rolls, cook until reduced by at least half.

Mix the remaining stock with the tomato purée and mustard and pour this over the rolls. Cover and cook over a medium-low heat, stirring occasionally and adding water if the sauce becomes too thick, for about 30–40 minutes. Remove the rolls and set aside in another pan over a low heat with some of the sauce to prevent them from drying out.

Stir the flour into the tomato sauce, add the crème fraîche, the chives or dill and season. Heat and stir until thickened. Pour the sauce over the cabbage rolls and serve with more crème fraîche and dill.

CHIPOTLE ROASTED VEGETABLES

with chilli beans & soured cream

A big plate of Mexican roasted veggies is pretty much my idea of comfort nirvana. The best bit is that it doesn't leave you feeling like you've got half a cow expanding in your guts for hours afterwards. This achieves the double whammy of decimating your veg box as well as fully utilising those hard to reach kitchen cupboard areas.

Serves 4

2.5kg mixed root vegetables (sweet potato, baking potato, pumpkin, parsnip, carrots), chopped into equal-sized wedges
2 teaspoons dried oregano
2 teaspoons smoked paprika
2 teaspoons ground cumin
4 fat garlic cloves, crushed
3 teaspoons chipotle paste
juice of 1 lime
2 teaspoons cocoa powder
2 teaspoons salt
4 tablespoons olive oil

1 medium onion, finely chopped
400g can mixed beans in chilli sauce
400g can chopped tomatoes
150ml chicken or vegetable stock
150ml soured cream
2 tablespoons finely chopped fresh coriander
2 green pickled chillies, finely chopped
1 tablespoon finely chopped red onion
freshly ground black pepper
grated Cheddar cheese and guacamole, to serve

Preheat the oven to 160°C/gas mark 3.

Arrange the root vegetables in a roasting tin. Whisk together the oregano, paprika, cumin, crushed garlic, chipotle paste, lime juice, cocoa powder, salt and 3 tablespoons of the olive oil in a bowl. Smear half this spice paste over the vegetables and roast them for 40–60 minutes or until all the vegetables are roasted and cooked through.

Meanwhile, heat the remaining olive oil in a medium pan, fry the onion and stir in the remaining spice paste. Tip in the beans. Stir in the tomatoes and stock and cook uncovered over a medium-low heat for about 40 minutes, until quite viscous and well flavoured.

Place the soured cream, coriander, chillies, red onion and black pepper in a small serving bowl and stir well to combine. Serve the roasted vegetables with the beans piled over and the chilli-coriander soured cream, grated Cheddar and guacamole on the side.

TUNA & PISTACHIO FISHCAKES

with beetroot & carrot remoulade

This is my mum's recipe and it's one of those dishes that everyone demands the recipe for. In Bangladesh they're made with fresh river fish, but canned tuna is perfectly able to withstand the headstrong attitude of garlic, ginger and coriander just as well, if not better. A real keeper this one, the pistachio nuts add a buttery crunch, but add whatever nuts you have to hand. Equally delicious cold in a lunch box or hot from the pan, with a delicate dollop of beetroot and carrot remoulade.

Makes 10-12

For the remoulade
4 tablespoons mustard mayonnaise
2 tablespoons crème fraîche
1 tablespoon lemon juice
2 tablespoons finely chopped fresh parsley
  or chives

1 small garlic clove, crushed
1½ tablespoons each of roasted sunflower
  seeds and roasted pumpkin seeds
2–3 beetroot, grated
2 carrots, grated

Whisk together all the remoulade ingredients and season to taste. Chill.

For the fishcakes
3 medium potatoes (about 350g),
  peeled and chopped
2 garlic cloves, crushed
2.5cm piece fresh root ginger, grated
1 tablespoon finely chopped fresh coriander
1 teaspoon curry powder
½ fresh green chilli (optional)
1 teaspoon cumin

½ onion, roughly chopped
198g can tuna in oil, drained
salt and freshly ground black pepper
2 eggs, beaten
50g pistachios, roughly chopped
2-3 tablespoons plain flour
100g panko breadcrumbs
250ml vegetable oil, for shallow frying
green salad, to serve

Place the potato chunks in a pan of boiling salted water, cook for 15–20 minutes or until tender. Drain and mash the potatoes and set aside.

Blitz the garlic, ginger, coriander, curry powder, chilli, cumin and onion with a touch of water to a thick emerald paste in a mini blender or food processor. Transfer to a large mixing bowl. Mix the drained tuna and mash into the spice paste. Add 1 teaspoon of salt and mix well with the potatoes, 1 beaten egg and pistachios. Check and adjust the seasoning if necessary.

Place the flour, breadcrumbs and remaining egg in 3 separate shallow bowls. With floured hands, shape the fishcake mixture into 10–12 smallish cakes, dip them in egg, then flour and then in the breadcrumbs.

Heat the oil in a large, non-stick frying pan over a medium heat and cook the fishcakes in batches of 4 for 5-6 minutes on each side or until golden all over. Remove from the pan with a slotted spoon and drain on kitchen paper. Serve the hot fish cakes with a sprightly green salad and a spoonful of chilled remoulade on the side.

BANOFFEE & ROSEMARY PIE

yum!

Condensed caramel is one of those filthily indulgent cans of utter lushness that no self-respecting kitchen cupboard should ever be without. Easy to whip up, the sophistication factor is taken up a gear with a hint of rosemary and a sprinkling of sea salt, to stop things becoming too sickly sweet.

Serves 4-6

200g ginger oaty biscuits
50g pecan or hazelnuts
75g butter, melted, plus extra for greasing
5–6 sprigs rosemary, leaves finely chopped
397g caramel condensed milk
1 teaspoon crushed sea salt
50g dark chocolate, broken into pieces

300ml double cream
1 teaspoon vanilla extract
1 tablespoon icing sugar
3 large bananas
juice of ½ small lime
cherries dipped in melted ginger chocolate,
    to decorate

Preheat the oven to 180°C/gas mark 4. Line a 20cm loose-bottomed cake tin with greased, crumpled baking parchment (this helps to keep the pie in place).

Crush the biscuits and nuts to a sandy rubble using a food processor and stir in the melted butter. Press this into the lined tin. Bake for 10 minutes until set and then leave to cool.

Stir the rosemary into the caramel condensed milk and spread over the base (don't overbeat as this will make the caramel too runny). Sprinkle over the crushed sea salt. Chill for at least 1 hour.

Just before serving, place the chocolate in a heatproof bowl over a pan of gently simmering water, stir until melted. Whip the cream, vanilla extract and icing sugar to soft peaks. Slice the bananas, pour over the lime juice and arrange over the caramel. Spoon generous drifts of the cream over this and drizzle over the chocolate. Decorate with the ginger chocolate cherries. Enjoy!

STEM GINGER, CHERRY & ALMOND FAT RASCALS

whoop!

This is an excellent little pud to have up your sleeve for those unexpected days of thrift and immobility. A cross between a scone and a bun, Fat Rascals originated in Yorkshire and date all the way back to Elizabethan times. They're fantastic for curing that 3.30pm sugar slump, and are also quite rich; so the ginger and cherries add balancing touches of spike and edge.

Makes 8

100g butter plus extra for greasing
150g self-raising flour
100g plain flour
1½ teaspoons baking powder
75g golden caster sugar
75g currants
75g sultanas
75g dried sour cherries

zest of 1 orange
zest of 1 lemon
6 nuggets of stem ginger in syrup,
    drained and chopped
½ teaspoon freshly grated nutmeg
250ml double cream
1 egg, beaten
60g flaked almonds and 8 dried sour
    cherries, to decorate

Preheat the oven to 220°C/gas mark 7. Grease 2 baking sheets.

Rub the butter into the flours and baking powder until you get the consistency of fine breadcrumbs.

Add the sugar, dried fruit, citrus zests, ginger and nutmeg and stir to combine well.

Add the cream and mix roughly to form a soft, pliable dough. Divide the dough into 8 equal pieces. Roll the dough into rounds and place on the greased baking sheets. Ensure they are well spaced as they have a tendency to spread! Brush with beaten egg, decorate with the remaining cherries and the almonds and bake for 15–20 minutes until golden brown. Transfer to a wire rack to cool.

These will keep for up to 2-3 days in an airtight container.

SALTED PEANUT BUTTER & CHOCOLATE CHIP COOKIES

mmm!

Always a winner, there are few things more enticing or endorphin inducing than a tray full of these cooling on your counters. The raw dough freezes superbly, which means you no longer have to worry about schlepping to the corner shop for a packet of those fake-flavoured hydrogenated oil versions next time you're after something to dunk in your cuppa. Bung a load of this dough in the freezer and you're never more than 20 minutes away from the real thing.

Makes 24

115g butter
100g caster sugar
100g dark muscovado sugar
1 egg
1 teaspoon vanilla extract

250g plain flour
1 teaspoon baking powder
½ teaspoon salt
230g crunchy peanut butter
100g milk chocolate, broken up into chunks

Preheat the oven to 180°C/gas mark 4. Line 2 baking trays with baking parchment.

In a large mixing bowl, cream together the butter and sugars until light and fluffy. Add the egg, vanilla extract, flour, baking powder and salt and mix well. Stir in the peanut butter and chocolate chunks until you have a nice, thick dough.

Roll the dough into a sausage shape about 25cm long on a floured surface and slice into cookies about 1cm wide, using a very sharp knife. (You could also freeze it at this point. When you want to bake slice into discs and bake for 17–20 minutes.) Space the cookies out evenly on the lined baking trays.

Bake the cookies for 12–15 minutes – they should be pale gold. Cool on the tray, as they're really crumbly while hot. Once cooled, transfer to a wire rack and tuck in.

FEEDING TO
WOW!

Life can be so mean sometimes. There you are, brimming with the joys of the weekend, when suddenly 'boof' it slaps you like a wet gurnard around the chops. The future in-laws are due for dinner. In 2 hours. Before you start hyperventilating, take a deep breath, read the following ideas and fire up that hob.

A few X factor dishes up your sleeve are the absolute order of the day. Basically, there are always going to be times when you need to confidently slide that wow factor out of the oven, without resorting to tired old clichés. These are the dishes you turn to when you want to seriously impress. The ones that make your guests/future spouse/boss regard you with renewed respect.

Without stating the obvious, the main idea is to make everything as stress free for yourself as possible. You're aiming for laid back, seemingly effortless culinary brilliance. It's good to take an alternative approach to classic dishes. Egg and chips, made with panache and a wink can be way more impressive than all the wood-fired foie gras in the world.

Here you'll find dishes you can mostly prep up in advance, so there's minimal kitchen time before people arrive and more time to take the rubbish out/sort out your monobrow/hide the ashtray. They'll be blown away by your incredible Coronation duck, with all the flavours of the original but using the crispy Peking technique, and if even Dr Pepper ribs can't score you a promotion, then quite frankly it's time to start looking for another job...

SUPER DELUXE TRIPLE-COOKED CHIPS

with a truffle-fried duck egg & rosemary salt

Who needs filet mignon or caviar when all anyone ever really wants is a plate of egg and chips done really, really well? So much more fun than something that looks over fussed and like you've just been on some cordon bleugh course. If you want to keep it vegetarian try to get hold of coconut oil (it's dead cheap in ethnic shops) which has the perfect smoking point for deep frying, or rice bran oil. Based on the classic Heston Method, it seems like a mega-faff but after an initial parboil and a fry you can just forget about them until you're ready to serve. The duck egg is fried with truffle oil or if you're feeling super flash you can always invest in a lump of the real thing, you only need a few titchy shavings per egg.

Serves 4

1kg floury potatoes
beef dripping or a mixture of vegetable
    and coconut oil, for deep frying
salt
½ tablespoon finely chopped fresh rosemary
1 tablespoon oak smoked salt

2 teaspoons chipotle paste
2 tablespoons tomato ketchup
2-3 teaspoons white truffle oil
knob of butter
4 duck eggs
1 tablespoon grated Parmesan cheese
freshly ground black pepper

Wash and peel the potatoes and cut into chips 2-3cm wide. Place in a saucepan of cold water to prevent them turning black. Rinse to remove the starch.

Add fresh water to the saucepan and bring to the boil. Parboil the chips for 8 minutes, drain, pat dry and stick in the freezer in one layer on a baking tray for 30 minutes.

Once the chips are chilled, heat the dripping or oil in a large pan or deep fat fryer to 160°C. Deep fry the chips for 10 minutes so they cook through without browning. Drain on kitchen paper, lightly salt and pop back in the freezer.

Stir the rosemary through the oak smoked salt to infuse. Then mix the chipotle paste with the tomato ketchup.

When you're ready to serve, reheat the dripping or oil to 180°C (or drop in a cube of stale bread, it should brown in 25-30 seconds) and brown the chips for 7 minutes.

Heat the truffle oil and the butter in a large non-stick frying pan, crack in the eggs and fry (duck eggs take 8-10 minutes). Baste several times to ensure the egg whites are cooked through.

Drain the chips on kitchen paper. Serve the eggs sprinkled with the Parmesan, rosemary salt and black pepper and a pile of chips, plus a blob of the chipotle ketchup, a bottle of vinegar on the side and a glass of Champagne.

MISO BUTTER ROAST CHICKEN

I know, I know, not another roast chicken recipe I hear you groan. As if there aren't enough ways to roast a chicken in the world... but this one is seriously different. If you can marinade the chicken overnight in the flavoured butter, so much the better. Miso butter may sound a bit out there, but it works dreamily with roast chicken, without making you feel like you've gone all fusion-batty on your Sunday roast. The only problem is that the butter burns easily. After a lot of experimenting, I found that roasting it my way ensures a super-succulent, moist bird, saturated with crescendos of umami and the crispest, salty skin of absolute fantasy. Try it once and I guarantee you'll never cook your chook any other way.

Serves 4

3 spring onions, very finely chopped
4 fat garlic cloves, crushed
85g red miso paste
90g butter
1.9kg chicken, the best you can afford
3 fat carrots, roughly chopped
2 onions, quartered
1 bay leaf
4 medium potatoes, peeled and halved
400ml chicken stock
salt
roast potatoes, bubble and squeak or
    dauphinoise potatoes, to serve

Preheat the oven to 180°C/gas mark 4. Mash the spring onions, garlic, miso paste and butter into a paste.

Push your fingers between the chicken skin and flesh and push about half the mixture in this cavity, massaging well all over the bird. Smear the remaining paste inside the body cavity and over the top of the chicken.

In a roasting dish with a rack, place the carrots, onions, bay leaf and potatoes under the rack. Pour the stock all over the vegetables and place the chicken, miso side up; on top. Cover tightly with 3 or 4 large lengths of foil so it's completely airtight. Pop in the oven and roast for 2 hours.

After 2 hours, remove the foil, and scrape off any excess marinade from the skin. Turn very carefully upside down (the chicken will be almost unmanageably tender). Sprinkle the now upward facing underside with salt and turn the heat up to 200°C/gas mark 6. Return to the oven for about 30 minutes until the skin is crisp.

Turn the chicken over, being very, very careful not to break up the bird and brown on the other side. This may well be a two person job.

Remove and rest the chicken under some foil on a serving dish in the oven on a low heat while you make the gravy. Place the roasting dish on the hob, heat over a high heat until reduced and intense. Serve with roast potatoes, bubble and squeak or dauphinoise potatoes.

GENTLY SPICED POT-ROASTED RABBIT

Rabbit is a wonderful, economical alternative to the usual boring old farmyard animals. Get your butcher to joint it for you and try to avoid using a pre-frozen bunny if possible. Here the meat pot roasts to tender dreaminess with spices and dark ale. It's not exactly a curry as the flavours are quite muted. It resides in that soft focus district, somewhere between a casserole and a korma, with subtle surges of flavour from all that ale-bathing. A doddle to put together, this lets the oven do all the work while you crack on with more important things.

Serves 4

2 teaspoons ground cumin
1 heaped tablespoon fresh root ginger, finely chopped
4 garlic cloves, crushed
½ teaspoon mace
1 teaspoon curry powder
½ teaspoon turmeric
2 teaspoons ground coriander
150g Greek yogurt
½ rabbit, jointed and lopped into bite-size chunks
1 tablespoon oil
1 teaspoon mustard seeds
2 onions, finely chopped
2 bay leaves
1 dried red chilli
4 green cardamom pods
1 cinnamon stick
1 parsnip, diced
1 large carrot, diced
300ml dark beer
500ml chicken stock
1 teaspoon salt
1 teaspoon sugar
1 teaspoon garam masala
75g frozen peas
toasted almond flakes and chopped fresh coriander, to garnish
steamed brown basmati rice and green salad, to serve

The night before you want to eat, mix together the cumin, ginger, garlic, mace, curry powder, turmeric and coriander with 2 tablespoons of the yogurt. Transfer to a shallow dish, add the rabbit pieces, stir to coat well, cover and refrigerate overnight.

The next day, preheat the oven to 180°C/gas mark 4. Heat the oil in a large, flameproof casserole and add the mustard seeds. Once they've popped add the onions, bay leaves, chilli, cardamom pods, and cinnamon stick and cook for a couple of minutes. Then tip in the rabbit pieces, browning well.

Stir in the diced parsnip and carrot and slosh in the beer. Cook over a high heat stirring well until the ale reduces a little. Pour in the chicken stock. Place the lid on and cook in the oven for 2–2½ hours or until the rabbit is spoonably tender.

Stir in the salt, sugar and garam masala and the remaining yogurt. Add the peas and cook for a further 5 minutes.

Garnish with the almonds and coriander. Serve with steamed brown basmati and a green salad.

CORONATION CRISPY DUCK

quack!

A real best of both worlds this one, combining all the flavour of coronation chicken with the sublime texture of crispy duck. You don't have to spend a fortune on a whole bird either, just a couple of legs are fine for two. A win win recipe if ever there was one, you get all the poaching and drying sorted the night before, and then it's just a blast in the oven while you whip up the spiced yogurt the next day. A guaranteed wow to the power of mmmm.

Serves 2

For the curry salt
1 teaspoon curry powder, toasted

1 teaspoon salt
2 duck legs

For the curry salt, toast the curry powder in a hot, non-stick, dry frying pan until fragrant, mix with 1 teaspoon salt. Pat the duck legs dry and rub them all over with the curry salt. Cover and chill in the fridge until you're ready to cook.

For the poaching liquid
2 cloves
1 cinnamon stick
30g fresh root ginger, unpeeled and chopped
1 heaped teaspoon black peppercorns
½ teaspoon mace

1 bay leaf
2 garlic cloves
¼ onion, roughly chopped
½ teaspoon turmeric
salt

Place all the poaching liquid ingredients in a pan of water, season with salt, and poach the duck legs for 40 minutes until tender. Remove and cool the legs (freeze the stock for a tasty laksa or dhal base).

Preheat the oven to 160°C/gas mark 3. Place the legs in a small roasting tin and roast them for 15-20 minutes until crisp.

For the spiced yogurt
30g fresh root ginger, finely chopped
30g walnuts, roughly chopped
1½ teaspoons curry powder
3 small spring onions
¼ red onion
60g ready-to-eat dried apricots,
    finely chopped

40g dried sour cherries
4 tablespoons mango chutney
2 teaspoons Worcestershire sauce
125g Greek yogurt
1 tablespoon mayonnaise
1 tablespoon tamarind sauce
finely chopped fresh coriander and
    toasted flaked almonds, to serve

Toast the ginger, walnuts and curry powder in a hot, non-stick, dry frying pan until fragrant. Transfer to a serving dish and add the remaining spiced yogurt ingredients. Stir well and sprinkle with the coriander and almonds. Serve this spooned generously alongside the duck legs to really max out the contrasts of crisp and creamy, hot and cold.

COURGETTE, PEA AND SMOKED DUCK CARBONARA

You can pick up smoked duck breast in some of the posher supermarkets, however, as it's a rare but pricy treat, it's a good idea stretch it out with carbs. Fresh yet smoky, the duck makes a fantastic alternative to the usual porcine protein in a carbonara. A great one for when you don't have that much time, but are keen to bring something a little bit different to the table.

Serves 4

For the carbonara
salt
500g penne or spaghetti
4 egg yolks
2 tablespoons soured or double cream
100g Pecorino or Parmesan cheese, grated
freshly ground black pepper
1 smoked skin on duck breast, sliced
    into strips

olive oil, for frying (optional)
1 garlic clove, chopped finely
2 courgettes, sliced into batons
100g frozen petits pois
2-3 tablespoons fresh thyme leaves or fresh
    chopped parsley
freshly grated nutmeg, to season
    (optional)

Bring a large pan of salted water to the boil. Cook the pasta according to the packet instructions.

While that's cooking mix the egg yolks, cream, and half the grated cheese together, season well.

In a medium frying pan, fry the duck breast until crisp. You shouldn't need any oil as the duck provides its own fat, but feel free to add a drop or two if you think it's looking dry.

Add the garlic and courgette batons and continue to stir and cook until the courgettes take on a golden tone and have lost their rawness. Throw in the peas and thyme or parsley, stir thoroughly and once everything is cooked, turn off the heat.

The pasta should have cooked by now, so drain it and reserve a little of the cooking water. Return the pasta to the pan and stir in the duck and vegetables. Stir in the egg mixture, allowing the heat from the pasta, plus the extra cooking water, if necessary, to form a silky emulsion. Stir in the remaining cheese, season well with black pepper and nutmeg and serve immediately.

For the salad
1 blood orange, peeled and pith removed
100g hazelnuts, toasted

100g spinach
olive oil and lemon juice, for drizzling
salt

To make the salad segment the blood orange and combine with the hazelnuts and spinach. Drizzle over the olive oil and lemon juice and season with salt.

LAMB MANTIS (TURKISH RAVIOLI)
with yogurt butter sauce

Authentic recipes for this Turkish ravioli in yogurt butter sauce call for making your own ravioli type dough. Personally, I think life's too short and have had some fantastic results using defrosted wonton wrappers from my local oriental supermarket instead. It's also important to use the fattier, cheaper cuts of lamb for this or the dish will be too dry. The yogurt butter sauce is what really elevates matters, along with the sumac and some fresh dill fronds... you can almost picture yourself in the back streets of Istanbul (or N16 as the case may be).

Serves 4

1 tablespoon olive oil, plus extra for oiling
1 onion, finely diced
1 medium aubergine, finely diced
235g finely chopped or minced fatty neck of lamb
2 teaspoons ground cumin
½ teaspoon freshly grated nutmeg
1 teaspoon ground cinnamon
paprika
1 teaspoon salt
1 teaspoon freshly ground black pepper
1 tablespoon chopped fresh parsley

2 teaspoons pomegranate molasses, plus extra to serve
20 wonton wrappers
500ml chicken stock
1 cinnamon stick
2 garlic cloves, crushed
1 small bunch fresh dill, finely chopped
250ml natural yogurt
50g butter, melted and the sediment skimmed off
1 teaspoon cayenne pepper
1 teaspoon dried sumac

Heat the oil in a large non-stick frying pan and fry the onion for 10 minutes until soft. Add the aubergine, lamb, half the cumin and the nutmeg, cinnamon and paprika. Cook for 15 minutes. Remove from the heat, season with the salt and pepper and stir in the parsley and pomegranate molasses. Leave to cool.

Put something absorbing on the telly and fill the wontons by placing heaped teaspoons of the lamb mix in one half of the wrapper, folding over to form a crescent shape and sealing with water, pinching well to ensure the mixture doesn't escape. Brush each one with oil to stop them from drying out.

Place the chicken stock, the remaining cumin, cinnamon stick and half the garlic in the base of a steamer and steam the dumplings in batches of 5-6 for around 15-20 minutes until tender and the wontons are cooked through, the pastry should be very soft. (I use a large saucepan, a sieve and a lid with excellent results.) Take care not to overcrowd the steamer as the wontons tend to clump together. Put the cooked wontons in a warm oven with a baking sheet of water in the bottom to prevent them drying out while you cook the rest.

Stir the remaining garlic and the dill into the yogurt. Serve the mantis with a little of the stock spooned over, a lavish blob of the dill yogurt, a trickle of the melted butter, a slick of pomegranate molasses and a dusting of cayenne and sumac.

LAMB SHANKS IN SHERRY

with roasted kale & salt-baked celeriac mash

Once the pride of every gastropub in the land, lamb shanks seem to have faded out of fashion. I love them braised for hours with a ton of vegetables. Crisp, roasted kale leaves are the perfect sidekick to this soothing respite in a bowl.

Serves 2

For the lamb
½ tablespoon smoked paprika
1 teaspoon salt
1 teaspoon dried oregano
1 teaspoon dried mint
1 teaspoon dried thyme
1 tablespoon chopped fresh rosemary
freshly ground black pepper

2 lamb shanks
2 tablespoons olive oil
2 carrots, diced
2 celery sticks, diced
3 onions, finely chopped
6 garlic cloves, chopped
1 star anise
250ml sherry or port
500ml lamb stock

Preheat the oven to 180°C/gas mark 4. Combine the smoked paprika, salt, oregano, mint, thyme and rosemary in a shallow dish, and season with black pepper. Place the lamb in the spice and herb mixture and turn to coat. Heat the oil in a large flameproof casserole and brown the coated lamb on all sides in the hot oil. Set aside.

Sauté the carrots, celery, onions, garlic and star anise for about 10 minutes in the same pan, then turn the heat up and deglaze the pan with the sherry or port.

Return the lamb to the casserole and pour in enough stock to cover. Stir well and once it's bubbling, cover and pop in the oven for 3 hours until fall-off-the-bone-at-the-mere-suggestion-of-a-spoon tender.

Remove the lamb shanks from the casserole and keep warm in a low oven. Strain the remaining sauce back into the casserole, pressing the veggies well to extract maximum flavour. Simmer until reduced and syrupy.

For the celeriac mash
2-3 egg whites
700g table salt
1 tablespoon finely chopped fresh chives
    or parsley

1 celeriac
3 floury potatoes unpeeled and scrubbed
olive oil, for mashing
smoked paprika and sea salt, to season

Combine the egg whites, salt and chives or parsley until you have a thick paste. Smear this all over the celeriac, so it's about 2cm thick, covering well and ensuring there aren't any gaps. Prick the potatoes. For the final hour, pop the celeriac and potatoes in the oven with the lamb.

To make the mash, chip open the salt crust, scoop out the celeriac and spoon the potato flesh from the skins. Mash the celeriac with the potato in a bowl, adding enough olive oil to make a creamy mash, season to taste with a smidge of smoked paprika and sea salt.

For the kale
200g kale
2 tablespoons olive oil

1 garlic clove, crushed
sea salt

Cut out and discard any woody ribs from the kale. Wash and dry the leaves thoroughly in a salad drier or with kitchen towel. Spread the kale in a single layer in a baking tray, mix well with the olive oil and the garlic and roast for the final 20 minutes of the lamb cooking time. Check it after 12 minutes or so – you should have crisp, papery leaves, but you don't want them to burn or they'll turn bitter. Stir frequently to ensure even roasting and once they're super crisp and dark green, sprinkle generously with sea salt and mix well. Serve the shanks with the celeriac and potato mash, crispy kale and the sauce and veg from the casserole.

BBQ BEEF RIBS

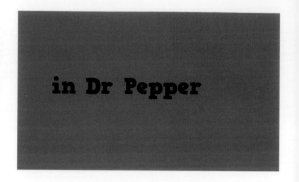

in Dr Pepper

These are mind-blowingly good. I love them so much I can never wait for BBQ season and just whack them in the oven in the middle of winter. Don't worry about the pop being sickly sweet in the finished dish - it tenderises the meat beautifully and renders down to an indeterminate tangy sticky moreishness. In fact, no one can ever identify quite what that 'mystery ingredient' actually is...

Serves 4

For the rub
3 garlic cloves
1 tablespoon salt
25 twists of freshly ground black pepper
1 tablespoon dark brown sugar
1 tablespoon honey mustard or Dijon mustard

½ teaspoon cayenne pepper
2 teaspoons chipotle paste
½ teaspoon paprika
1 tablespoon Worcestershire sauce
1 teaspoon dried oregano
1 teaspoon dried thyme

The night before you want to eat, rinse the ribs and pat them dry. Crush the garlic to a paste with the salt. Combine the garlic paste with the remaining rub ingredients and smear over the meat. Cover and refrigerate overnight, meat side up in a lidded casserole.

For the ribs
1800g-2kg beef short ribs

500ml Dr Pepper

The next day remove the casserole from the fridge and allow the ribs to come to room temperature. Preheat the oven to 180°C/gas mark 4. Pour the Dr Pepper over the marinated ribs, cover tightly with foil and a lid and roast for 2 hours.

For the glaze
500ml Dr Pepper
4 tablespoons tomato ketchup
4 tablespoons Dijon mustard
150ml cider vinegar

1 onion, grated
3 garlic cloves, crushed
90ml soy sauce
mashed potatoes and peas, to serve

Place all the glaze ingredients in a small pan and simmer over a very low heat for 1 hour – it should still be very soupy but quite glossy. After 2 hours remove the ribs from the oven and transfer to a roasting tin, meat side down. Pour over all the juices from the casserole and spread 3-4 tablespoons of the glaze on each side of the meat. It will still look quite 'liquidy' at this stage, but don't worry.

Place back in the oven and cook, uncovered, for a further hour. Keep smearing with more of the glaze every half an hour for about 4-5 hours. The meat should be immersed in a fair amount of liquid and you should be able to just flake it away with a spoon by the end.

To make the gravy, rest the ribs, covered in foil. Pour off the excess oil and heat the roasting tray of juices and glaze on the hob. Add 1 tablespoon plain flour and stir until nice and thick.

TERIYAKI RICE 'BURGERS'

with miso special sauce

I first came across these when I lived in the land of the rising sun. I remember thinking they perfectly epitomised everything I loved about that crazy, futuristic yet traditional country. They're basically two burger 'buns' made from fried rice patties with a teriyaki beef filling. My miso burger sauce is one those maddeningly tasty little condiments that you just cannot get enough of, and makes the finished dish a bit of a triumph. They are a great example of how good the Japanese are at taking a Western classic and making it their very own.

Serves 2

For the miso burger sauce
2 tablespoons tomato ketchup
1 tablespoon miso paste
4 tablespoons mayonnaise

Combine all the miso burger sauce ingredients in a small bowl and stir well. Set aside.

For the rice 'burgers'
3 teaspoons soy sauce
3 teaspoons sake
3 teaspoons rice vinegar
3 teaspoons mirin
3 teaspoons sugar
5cm piece fresh root ginger, finely grated
3 garlic cloves, crushed in a garlic crusher
265g rump steak, very thinly sliced
290g Japanese-style medium grain sushi rice
salt and freshly ground black pepper
1 tablespoon sesame oil
2 tablespoons olive oil
2 nori sheets
lettuce, fried onion rings and Japanese pickled mushrooms (optional), to serve

The night before or at least 2 hours before you want to start cooking, mix the soy sauce, sake, rice vinegar, mirin, sugar, ginger and garlic in a shallow bowl. Stir in the steak slices and refrigerate. Rinse the rice in a sieve and set aside to absorb any excess water for 30 minutes.

Place the rice in a pan with 350ml water, bring to the boil, simmer for 10 minutes and turn heat off. Allow to steam with the lid on for a further 10 minutes, cool slightly and season. Line a 10cm ramekin with lightly oiled clingfilm, press one quarter of the hot rice firmly into the bottom and turn out onto clingfilm. Repeat to give you 4 perfect burger bun shapes, then refrigerate.

Warm up a frying pan or wok and heat half the sesame and olive oils. Strain the beef and fry it over a very high heat for around 4-6 minutes, depending on how well-done you like it. Stir the slices to ensure it cooks evenly. Add the remaining oils and in the same pan fry the patties on each side until a light brown crust is formed. Cut the nori sheets into the same circular shape as the buns and line each bun with a circle of nori as it comes out of the pan. This will form a protective seal around the rice and minimise the 'crumble' factor.

Place mounds of the teriyaki beef in between each of the nori-lined rice buns and top with a hefty dollop of the miso burger sauce. Add a lettuce leaf, fried onion ring, a teaspoon of Japanese pickled mushrooms and serve immediately with a chilled Asian beer.

ROASTED NECTARINE & PINEAPPLE RUM RAISIN ICE CREAM

fruity!

You don't often see rum and raisin ice cream anymore do you? It's one of those childhood combos that conjures up so much more than yearnings for the taste. It's also the fact that it harboured that mysterious, forbidden and therefore extra delicious ingredient: rum. In the same way shandy or ginger beer or those little confectionary cigarettes with a pink 'fire' dot painted on the end that you pretended to smoke before snaffling, were coveted. Rich, caramel notes plus a juicy fruit bass line make this a real treat. Any type of rum you can get hold of will work fine and peaches are just as good as nectarines.

Serves 8

3 nectarines or peaches, halved and stoned
1 pineapple, peeled, corec, sliced into rings
    and quartered
50g muscovado sugar
50g butter
250ml whole milk
100g caster sugar

pinch of salt
seeds from ½ vanilla pod or
    1 teaspoon vanilla extract
3 egg yolks, beaten
300ml double cream
150g raisins
100ml rum

Preheat the oven to 160°C/gas mark 3.

Place the nectarines or peaches and the pineapple in a roasting tray, sprinkle with the muscovado sugar and dot with the butter. Roast for 1 hour.

Meanwhile place the milk, caster sugar, salt and vanilla seeds or extract in a small pan and heat until almost boiling. Remove from the heat, cool slightly and add the beaten egg yolks, mixing well until custard-like. Stir in the cream.

Heat the raisins and rum in a second small pan and macerate for 15 minutes, until the rum is absorbed into the fruit. Set aside to cool. Once completely cold, stir this into the creamy mixture, stirring everything really well.

Roughly chop the roasted fruit and stir it into the ice cream mix, making sure you also scrape in all the luscious, fruity caramel. Transfer to an ice-cream maker to freeze or transfer to an airtight, lidded container and pop in the freezer, stirring every 30 minutes for about 4 hours.

WARM LYCHEE, LIME & CARDAMOM TART

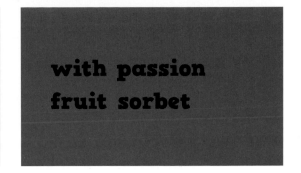

with passion fruit sorbet

I once fed this to a very hard to please, well-known food critic and he, a self-confessed lychee hater, grudgingly admitted he was turned (he went nuts for the sorbet!). The warm, perfumed tart with the sharp, citrus stab of icy tart passion fruit is a killer combo, but if you're really not keen you could always substitute a couple of chopped up bananas instead of the fragrant orbs.

Serves 6-8

For the sorbet
10 passion fruit
2 limes
150g caster sugar
1 tablespoon ginger syrup, from a jar
    of stem ginger (optional)

Scoop the pulp and seeds out of the passion fruit. Zest and juice the limes. Place 150ml water and the sugar in a small pan and simmer for 5-10 minutes until it forms a thin syrup. Pour this over the passion fruit along with the ginger syrup (if using). Pour half the lime juice (reserve the zest and remaining juice) into the syrup, and allow to cool slightly. Transfer the syrup to an ice-cream maker to freeze or place in an airtight, lidded container. Pop in the freezer and stir briskly every 30 minutes until frozen – this will take 1–2 hours.

For the pastry
150g butter
250g plain flour
1 tablespoon icing sugar
1 egg, beaten
pinch of salt

Place the butter, flour and icing sugar in a large mixing bowl and rub them together to form breadcrumbs. Add half the beaten egg and the salt and see if the mixture just comes together to form a dough. Add more egg if necessary. Line a 25cm flan dish with the pastry, prick lightly with a fork and freeze for 10-15 minutes or refrigerate for 30 minutes.

Preheat the oven to 180°C/gas mark 4. Cover the pastry with baking parchment and baking beans or lentils and bake blind for 30 minutes, then remove the paper and beans and bake for a further 10 minutes to brown slightly. Set the baked pastry shell aside to cool. Once cooled, line with the lychee halves.

For the filling
13 fresh lychees, halved
4 green cardamom pods
3 eggs
100g caster sugar
1 teaspoon vanilla extract
200g double cream
fresh mint leaves, to garnish

Remove the cardamom seeds from the pods and grind them using a pestle and mortar. Whisk together the ground cardamom, eggs, reserved lime juice and zest, sugar and vanilla extract in a bowl until well blended. Beat in the cream and transfer to a large jug. Place the pastry shell on a baking tray and carefully pour in the cream. Bake for 30-35 minutes or until just set in the centre. It should give a slight wobble when removed. Garnish with the mint leaves and serve the tart warm with a scoop of sorbet.

PINK GRAPEFRUIT MERINGUE PIE

delish!

Pink grapefruit is massively underrated and here it makes a fine alternative to the usual lemon curd filling. You need to eat this on the day you make it really, so if you need to, make the base and the filling in advance and just sort the meringue out on the day.

Serves 6-8

For the pastry
butter, for greasing
250g plain flour
70g icing sugar
zest of 2 limes
125g butter, diced
1 egg
2 tablespoons milk

Preheat the oven to 200°C/gas mark 6 and stick a baking sheet in there to warm. Grease a 23cm pie dish with butter.

Place the flour, icing sugar, lime zest and diced butter in a large mixing bowl and rub them together to form breadcrumbs. Add the egg and milk and bring together to form a dough. Press the pastry into the greased dish, up the sides and ensure there's plenty of overhang. You want it to be fairly thin. Prick lightly with a fork and refrigerate for 15 minutes.

Cover the pastry with baking parchment and baking beans and bake blind for 15 minutes and then uncovered for a further 5 minutes to brown slightly. Set the baked pastry shell aside to cool. Reduce the oven temperature to 160°C/gas mark 3.

For the filling
180g caster sugar
6 eggs
200ml double cream
zest and juice of 1 pink grapefruit

For the filling, separate 4 of the eggs and place the whites in a grease-free bowl. Whisk the caster sugar, 2 whole eggs and 4 egg yolks, double cream, grapefruit zest and juice in a bowl until blended. Transfer to a jug. Place the pastry case in the oven shelf and carefully pour in the filling. Bake for 30-35 minutes until set. Trim the pastry and leave to cool. Increase the oven temperature to 180°C/gas mark 4.

For the meringue
2 teaspoons cornflour
115g caster sugar
115g icing sugar

To make the meringue whisk the egg whites until they form stiff peaks. Add the cornflour and the caster sugar 1 tablespoonful at a time and continue to whisk until the peaks are much stiffer. Slowly sift in the icing sugar, being careful not to overmix.

Top the cooled pie with peaks of the meringue – place spoonfuls around the edge so it just touches the pastry (this will prevent slippage). Swirl the rest in the middle and bake for 15-20 minutes, until the peaks are crisp and golden. Resist the urge to open the oven door and check it! Turn the heat off and allow the pie to cool in the oven. If you can wait, this is best left for an hour before slicing to serve.

TICK TOCK,
TICK TOCK...

While it's all very well being instructed to hang about for hours while your sourdough elevates, in reality most of us barely have time to wolf down last night's leftovers once we've bombed in from the electronic coalface and need to rush straight back out again. It's helpful to have recipes that you can throw together without too much hassle, you know, IRL.

We seem to be eating out and relying on fast food more than ever. But fast food doesn't necessarily have to manifest itself in a greasy bag of bovine horror. Being time skint doesn't always have to mean grazing on rubbish. It can be as simple as a cheese and sage omelette sarnie, something exciting on toast or a bowl of chicken noodle soup, made in the time it takes to heat up a quick tangle of carbs in some chicken stock and miso.

If you can, thinking and planning ahead means you can still tuck into a plate of umami rich aubergine, rice and pickles. Or a muesli bar, studded with a halo of pumpkin seeds and a pitchfork of chocolate peanut butter gleefully devoured on the hop. If you don't have time to plan what to eat, then just stash the necessary basics in your cupboard or freezer and you'll be rewarded with a plumper wallet and fast food on tap, made exactly the way you like it.

SUPER FAST KIMCHI PICKLED MELON

A fermented Korean dish made with a variety of vegetables, this pungent pickle is also regarded as a bit of a health food because of its high vitamin content. I was taught to make kimchi by a Korean model turned English teacher in Japan. Her nan used to make huge vats of it in clay pots and then bury them in the garden like time capsules for aeons, to really ferment. It's pungent stuff kimchi, but also maddeningly addictive. Traditionally used to pickle cabbage, I find the sweet-savoury combo with melon creates a real riot of flavour, and bypasses some of the more sulphuric notes of the brassica version. This is ready in about half an hour, so just enough time to steam up a bowl of jasmine rice and some mixed vegetable miso soup. You could also try it slipped inside a cheeseburger for an exciting twist.

Serves 4

½ cantaloupe or honeydew melon, diced
1 teaspoon salt
1 teaspoon finely chopped garlic
½–1 teaspoon chilli powder (I like to use
   Korean gochugaru)

1 spring onion
1 teaspoon sugar
2 teaspoons rice vinegar
1 teaspoon sesame oil
1 tablespoon roasted sesame seeds

Combine all the ingredients in an airtight lidded container and mix well to coat the melon. Leave to infuse for 30 minutes.

This will keep for about 3 days in the airtight container in the fridge.

WOK-FRIED AUBERGINE & TOFU STIR FRY
with Szechuan sauce

One of the most dog-eared, oil spattered books amongst my cookery collection is Fuchsia Dunlop's Sichuan Cookery. It totally demystifies the cuisine and her recipes are pretty much idiot-proof. This recipe is inspired by her classic Fish Fried Aubergine. Unbelievably speedy, this is way more thrilling than your average stir fry.

Serves 4

2 tablespoons rice bran or sunflower oil
2 small aubergines, cut into 3mm-thick slices
1 teaspoon sesame oil
2–3 garlic cloves, crushed
1 tablespoon finely chopped fresh root ginger
350g firm tofu, drained and diced
3 teaspoons chilli bean paste

3 teaspoons soy sauce
3 teaspoons mirin
2 teaspoons Shaoxing rice wine
2 handfuls of pak choy, cabbage or
    spinach, shredded
1 teaspoon sugar
3 spring onions, finely chopped
steamed rice, to serve

Heat the oil in a wok or large frying pan and shallow fry the aubergine slices for 15-20 minutes, turning over halfway, and cook until they are tender and golden. Remove using a slotted spoon and drain on kitchen paper.

Add the sesame oil, garlic, ginger and tofu chunks to the wok and continue to fry for 10-15 minutes or until the tofu is well browned. Add the chilli bean paste, soy sauce, mirin and rice wine to the pan and stir fry for 5 minutes until the paste is fragrant.

Return the aubergines to the pan and stir to coat well. Add the greens and cook for a further minute or two.

Finally sprinkle over the sugar and spring onions and serve with plenty of steamed rice.

WALNUT MISO AUBERGINE SLICES

wow!

If you're sick of paying through the nose for your nasu dengaku in fancy restaurants, then look no further. In this version the walnuts add a glorious nutty crunch in contrast to the general notion of creamy flavour, but if you don't have any you can always leave them out. This is perfect for when you're dashing out the door, it's ready in two shakes of a lamb's tail (or at least no more time than it takes to cook up a pan of rice). And if you've an extra 5 minutes you can make your own quick pickled cucumbers by tossing chunks in salt, sugar and rice vinegar before preparing the aubergines.

Serves 4

2 tablespoons miso paste
2 teaspoons soy sauce
2 teaspoons sugar
2 tablespoons sake
2 tablespoons mirin

30g finely crushed walnuts
2–3 oriental aubergines or 1–2 standard
    aubergines
4 tablespoons vegetable oil
2 spring onions, finely chopped
rice and pickled cucumber, to serve

Whack the grill up to high. In a small bowl, mix the miso, soy sauce, sugar, sake, mirin and walnuts until the sugar completely dissolves.

Slice the aubergine into discs and heat 2 tablespoons of the oil in a pan. Shallow fry half the slices for 4–5 minutes on each side or until they are golden and tender. Drain the slices on kitchen paper and transfer to a baking sheet. Repeat with the remaining oil and aubergines. Slather the walnut miso over the aubergine slices.

Cook under the preheated grill for 1-2 minutes. Sprinkle over the spring onions and serve with rice and pickles.

WILD MUSHROOM, HERB & GARLIC SALT-BAKED EGGS

easy!

The internet is agog with recipes for flavoured salts and this is my one for wild mushroom and garlic. It's potent, transformative stuff, and brings out the best in almost any savoury dish, from steak to salad (it's the human equivalent of catnip in my Mushroom pâté recipe on page 160). I like to make a batch and store it somewhere airtight to sprinkle over pasta or rice salads for true Speedy Gonzales suppers. You can use any kind of dried mushroom, so whack in whatever you have/can afford (shiitake is interesting). This makes a truly satisfying starter or a simple meal, with a green salad and plenty of warm bread and butter.

Serves 2-4

For the wild mushroom salt
25g dried mushrooms
50g sea salt (I like to use smoked Maldon)

2 teaspoons dried parsley
2 teaspoons dried thyme
1–2 teaspoons garlic powder

In a spice mill, coffee grinder or pestle and mortar blitz the dried mushrooms and salt to a fine powder. Transfer to a small airtight lidded container and stir in the parsley, thyme and garlic powder and mix well.

For the eggs
butter, for greasing
200g spinach
freshly grated nutmeg, to season
freshly ground black pepper

4 eggs
3 tablespoons double cream
2 tablespoons grated Parmesan
green salad and warm bread and butter,
    to serve

Preheat the oven to 180°C/gas mark 4. Place 4 lightly buttered ramekin dishes in a roasting tin.

Place the spinach in a colander and pour boiling water over it to wilt it. Press the wilted spinach with the back of a spoon to squeeze it dry and then finely chop it.

Divide the spinach between the ramekin dishes and season with nutmeg and black pepper. Crack an egg into each dish.

Sprinkle the eggs liberally with the mushroom, garlic and herb salt (½–1 teaspoon per egg). Top each egg with a little cream and cover with cheese. Pour in enough boiling water into the roasting tin to come about one quarter of the way up the outsides of the ramekins. Bake for 10 minutes for a soft yolk or 15 minutes for something a bit firmer. Serve straight away with a green salad and warm bread and butter.

ROASTED OKRA
with spinach yogurt sauce

Okra seems to be a bit Marmite in the vegetable world – the gooey seeds are either adored or detested. I'm very much in the former camp myself, but for the texturally conservative, this recipe cuts down on the ooze factor nicely and is an absolute doddle to make. The spinach yogurt sauce adds a cool, creamy counteraction to the hot crisp okra. Tucked into a hot pitta or simply devoured with some salad and rice, this will leave your wallet, waistline and tastebuds filled with an incredible degree of smugness for staying strong and boycotting the dodgy kebab shop.

Serves 2

240g okra, stems trimmed
1 teaspoon salt
1 tablespoon olive oil
1 teaspoon cumin seeds
50g walnuts or pine nuts
1 garlic clove, crushed
250g spinach

250g Greek yogurt
1 teaspoon dried mint
salt and freshly ground black pepper
1 tablespoon chopped fresh parsley
1 tablespoon balsamic vinegar or
    pomegranate molasses
rice or pitta bread and pickled chillies,
    to serve

Preheat the oven to 200°C/gas mark 6.

Toss the okra with 1 teaspoon salt and the olive oil and arrange in a single layer in a roasting tin. Roast in the oven for about 15 minutes. The okra should be nicely seared but still tender.

Meanwhile, heat a pan. Dry fry the cumin seeds and walnuts or pine nuts until they are toasted. Add the garlic and stir in the spinach until it just wilts (a couple of minutes at most). Roughly shred the spinach mixture and allow it to cool.

Tip the cooled spinach into a bowl and stir in the yogurt and dried mint and season well.

Sprinkle the okra with the parsley and balsamic vinegar or pomegranate molasses and eat cold with rice or stuffed into hot pitta bread with the spinach and yogurt sauce and a pickled chilli or two on the side.

ROSE VEAL & SPINACH STROGANOFF

I was brought up to believe that dining on veal was something that only the most unethical, bloody minded cretinous type would indulge in. Horror stories of baby cows being butchered in the cruellest fashion abound and you might as well have been feasting on someone's newborn in front of them. Recently though, the debate has shifted, as the UK now produces some of the most ethically raised veal in Europe. Rose veal comes from happy cows, raised in accordance with the RSPCA's Freedom Food regulations.

Serves 2-4

25g butter
400g rose veal, cut into thin strips
1 onion, thinly sliced
2 garlic cloves, crushed
1 teaspoon paprika
1 teaspoon cayenne pepper
150g button chestnut mushrooms, sliced
120ml dry white wine
100ml soured cream

2 tablespoons Greek yogurt
freshly grated nutmeg, to season
1 teaspoon Worcestershire sauce
200g baby spinach
1 tablespoon chopped fresh parsley
1 tablespoon chopped fresh chives
salt and freshly ground black pepper
green salad with chopped gherkins
    and steamed wild rice, to serve

Heat the butter in a large, non-stick frying pan. Add the veal and fry over a high heat for a minute or two until browned. Remove the veal from the pan with a slotted spoon and set aside on a plate.

Add the onion, garlic, paprika, cayenne pepper and mushrooms to the frying pan and cook for 15 minutes over a low heat. Throw in the wine and increase the heat. Then cook for 2-3 minutes until reduced by half.

Return the veal and any juices to the pan with the soured cream, yogurt, nutmeg, Worcestershire sauce and spinach. Season well, stir and cook through until the spinach just wilts. Remove from the heat and stir in the parsley and chives. Serve immediately with a gherkin-ridden salad and lots of steamed wild rice.

SPICED ROE ON HOT BUTTERED TOAST

Serves 2-4

2 tablespoons plain flour
½ teaspoon turmeric
1 teaspoon curry powder
1 teaspoon salt
knob of butter plus extra for spreading
1 tablespoon vegetable oil

100g can cod roes
handful of watercress
1 tablespoon finely chopped parsley
1 shallot, finely chopped
2 slices of your favourite bread and butter,
   to serve
lemon juice, for squeezing

Mix the flour, turmeric, curry powder and salt together in a shallow bowl.

Heat the knob of butter and oil in a small, non-stick frying pan. Carefully dredge the roe in the seasoned flour, coating well and add to the sizzling pan. Fry over a medium heat for 2 minutes, allowing a dark golden crust to form, flip it over and cook for a further 2 minutes.

Combine the watercress, parsley and shallot to make a salad. Toast the bread and butter it generously. Divide pieces of the fried roe between the buttered toast, squeeze over some lemon juice and pile the salad on top and serve.

TERIYAKI TROUT

Serves 2-4

4 trout fillets

For the marinade
50ml soy sauce
100ml mirin
100ml sake
2 tablespoons sesame oil

2 tablespoons rice vinegar
juice of ½ lime
3 spring onions, finely chopped
2cm piece fresh root ginger, grated
1 garlic clove, crushed
1 heaped teaspoon sugar
sushi rice salad cucumber and seaweed,
   to serve

Place the fish fillets in a shallow dish. Mix all the marinade ingredients together in a jug and pour over the fish fillets. Set aside to marinade for a minimum of 15 minutes but no longer than 30 minutes, to avoid toughening the fish.

Preheat the grill to high and grill the fillets for 3–4 minutes on each side. Serve with a salad of sushi rice, cucumber and seaweed.

SEAWEED & FENNEL BUTTER SOLE

with lentil & samphire salad

The seaweed-fennel butter is what really makes it, so do buy the best salted butter you can afford and look out for dried nori seaweed at the supermarket or from www.japancentre.com. Such a simple, classic way to cook fish, you'll find yourself making this on repeat and if you're literally running out of the door, you can make the lentil salad in advance. The fish takes minutes to cook and you don't have to use sole, it's also magic with scallops or a nice bit of dab. Samphire is a crisp, salty green sea vegetable which is available from most fishmongers, and increasingly from supermarkets.

Serves 2

½ teaspoon fennel seeds
100g butter
1 teaspoon salt
15–20g dried nori seaweed (hijiki flakes or wakame)
100g green lentils
500ml chicken or vegetable stock
handful of samphire (optional)

handful of frozen peas or frozen broad beans
1 beetroot, grated
½ fennel bulb, thinly sliced
20g Parmesan shavings
½ garlic clove, crushed
½ tablespoon lemon juice
1 tablespoon finely chopped fresh parsley
1 tablespoon olive oil
2 x 200g lemon sole fillets

Toast the fennel seeds in a hot, non-stick, dry frying pan until fragrant and grind to a powder using a pestle and mortar or in a spice mill or coffee grinder. Combine with the butter and salt in a food processor. Crush the nori to a powder using a pestle and mortar or in a spice mill or coffee grinder. Add to the butter in the processor and pulse until thoroughly blended. Cover and set aside.

Place the lentils and stock in a medium pan, bring to the boil and cook for 35–40 minutes or until tender. Add the samphire, peas or broad beans and boil for a further minute, or until tender. Drain and transfer to a serving dish. Stir the grated beetroot into the lentil mixture with the fennel and Parmesan. In a small jug, combine the garlic, lemon juice, parsley and olive oil to make a dressing.

Preheat the grill to medium high. Place the fish on a baking try and smear all over with the seaweed butter and grill for 3–4 minutes on each side.

Dress the lentil salad and serve with the fish and spoon over plenty of melted seaweed butter from the baking tray.

PINK GRAPEFRUIT MARINATED SALMON

with caper and dill yogurt dressing

Salmon can be so flabby and meh, sometimes you need to introduce the adrenaline of acid to really charge up the flavour and texture. If you want to make matters more substantial, you could throw in some boiled new potatoes. It's also pretty special in a wholemeal sandwich or wrap.

Serves 2

120g smoked salmon (also great with
    smoked trout or mackerel)
juice of ½ pink grapefruit
½ red onion, finely chopped
1 tablespoon soy sauce

1 tablespoon rice vinegar
2 teaspoons capers in brine, drained and
    chopped
2 tablespoons natural yogurt
1 tablespoon dill fronds, finely chopped
freshly ground black pepper
2 little gem lettuces, shredded

Place the salmon in a shallow dish. Combine the grapefruit juice, red onion, soy sauce and rice vinegar and pour over the salmon. Leave for 20–30 minutes to semi-ceviche it.

In a small bowl mix the capers, yogurt, dill and black pepper.

Add the shredded lettuce to the salmon and stir to combine. Drizzle the yogurt dressing over the salmon mixture and serve.

GINGERED CRAB RAREBIT

snap! snap!

Welsh rarebit is such an underrated joy, as is a nice, icy alcoholic ginger beer. Here I've celebrated the two for a super fast and oozingly delicious stomach-liner of true champions. Traditionally made with ale or stout, I find the gingery notes of the beer combined with the subtle ozone of crab transforms it into something pretty special.

Serves 2

3 tablespoons alcoholic ginger beer
1 teaspoon grainy mustard
40g butter
50g Gruyère cheese, grated

a big dash Worcestershire sauce
salt and freshly ground black pepper
4 slices of bread, whatever you have to
    hand is fine
170g canned or fresh crabmeat
1 egg, beaten

Pour the ginger beer and mustard into a small pan. Add the butter and stir until it melts. Add the cheese, Worcestershire sauce, and seasoning to taste. Continue to cook until the cheese has completely melted.

Preheat the grill to high and lightly toast the bread on both sides. Once the bread is toasted, leave the grill on. Drain the crab and arrange on the toast.

Mix the egg into the cheesy-beer pan, off the heat, stirring until thickened. Pour this over the crab toast slices and grill for 5 minutes until golden and bubbling.

SPICED MUSSEL ONE POT WONDER

hot!

When it comes to fast food, mussels are like the jaguars of the food world — they literally cook in minutes and if you're really up against it, you could even cook the rice in advance, so all that's left to do is steam open the mussels and devour. Cheap, sustainable and unfeasibly delectable, this is one of my favourite weeknight dishes. It's especially good when it's all wintry outside, as every mouthful really conjures up the notion of balmy southern Indian evenings.

Serves 2-3

2kg mussels
40g butter
1 teaspoon mustard seeds
12–15 curry leaves
1 onion, finely chopped
3 bay leaves
2 garlic cloves, finely chopped
1 heaped teaspoon curry powder

½ teaspoon ground turmeric
200g brown basmati rice
1 teaspoon salt
300ml dry cider
60g creamed coconut
300ml boiling water
300ml vegetable stock
150g frozen peas
fresh coriander and fresh lime wedges,
   to serve

Check over the mussels, ripping out any beards, chucking away any that are broken, weirdly heavy, or that don't close when you give them a good tap against a hard surface. Stick the rest in a colander and wash them under cold running water for a couple of minutes.

Melt the butter in a large lidded saucepan. Once it foams and before it burns (!) throw in the mustard seeds and curry leaves. Once they've spat and crackled, add the onion, bay leaves, garlic, curry powder, turmeric, rice and salt. Turn up the heat, glug in the cider and reduce until dryish. Dissolve the creamed coconut in the boiling water and add it, with the stock, to the rice, reduce the heat and simmer until the rice is almost cooked through (15 minutes-ish).

Stir in the peas and cook for minute or two, until heated through. Clatter in the mussels, turn the heat up and pop the lid on. After about 5–7 minutes have a peek. They should all have opened wide – discard any that haven't.

Ladle the rice into warmed soup bowls, pile the mussels on top and strew liberally with the coriander and sprinkle with lime juice.

CRAYFISH LAKSA

wow!

The shop bought versions of laksa paste can be a bit lacking in oomph, so I like to combine mine with elements of a homemade one for an authentic slap of flavour. If you're really in a mad dash, then just blitz the paste ingredients up the night before. The paste really is the only time consuming part of this dish – it can also be made in advance and then frozen in ice cube trays, ready for whenever you feel the need to whip up a bowl of something nourishing and spicy.

Serves 2

For the paste
1 dessertspoon laksa or shrimp paste
2 green chillies
1 onion, roughly chopped
2 stems lemongrass (white part only), trimmed and chopped
2cm piece fresh root ginger, peeled and chopped
3 garlic cloves, crushed
2 teaspoons turmeric
2 tablespoons roughly chopped coriander leaves and stems
50g roasted peanuts

Blitz up all the paste ingredients in a food processor.

For the soup
1 tablespoon vegetable oil
1–2 tablespoons creamed coconut
1 litre boiling water
1 chicken stock cube
juice of ½ lime
1 teaspoon brown sugar
3 teaspoons Thai fish sauce
1 tablespoon soy sauce
2 x 250g nests of egg noodles
2 handfuls of beansprouts
500g raw crayfish tails
¼ cucumber, julienned
fresh coriander and mint, chopped
salt and chilli flakes
lime wedges, to serve

Heat the oil in a large pan and fry the paste for a couple of minutes. Dissolve the creamed coconut in the boiling water and add it to the pan with the chicken stock cube, lime juice, sugar, fish sauce and soy sauce and simmer for 15 minutes.

Meanwhile, cook the noodles according to the pack instructions and drain in a colander.

Taste and adjust the laksa, seasoning according to taste with more sugar, lime juice, fish sauce or soy sauce as necessary.

Pour boiling water over the noodles in the colander and divide them between two bowls. Top with the beansprouts.

Add the crayfish to the laksa and cook for a couple more minutes, or until they turn pink. Top the noodles with the crayfish and ladle in the soup. Garnish with cucumber, coriander and mint and season with salt and chilli flakes to taste. Serve with lime wedges.

PEANUT BUTTER & CHOCOLATE MUESLI BARS

sweet!

This very much hits that sweet spot, where health food meets guilty pleasure, and after a bit of experimenting I've finally come up with a most excellent ratio of chunky to sticky. Make them the night before if you know you've got a manic day ahead. Easily slipped into the pocket, these are the perfect little on-the-go snackette. Never again will you waste your cash on one of those overpriced over-sugared shop-bought versions. These little beauties last for about a week in an airtight lidded container in the fridge.

Makes 12 squares

butter, for greasing
30g sesame seeds
90g oats
65g sunflower seeds
110g sultanas

35g wheatgerm
100g butter
2–3 tablespoons clear honey
100g milk chocolate, broken into pieces
100g smooth peanut butter
1 teaspoon vanilla extract

Grease and line a 30cm x 22cm rectangular tin with baking parchment. Toast the sesame seeds in a hot, non-stick, dry frying pan until golden.

Mix the toasted sesame seeds, oats, sunflower seeds, sultanas and wheatgerm in a large mixing bowl. Stir well to combine.

Heat the butter, honey and chocolate in a small pan over a very gentle heat until the chocolate melts, make sure it does not burn. Remove from the heat and stir in the peanut butter and vanilla. Pour the melted mixture into the dry ingredients and stir well.

Spoon into the prepared baking tin and press it down with the back of a large metal spoon. Set aside to cool and then cut into 12 squares.

MEATLESS
MAGIC

If there's one tea time trauma I encounter time and again, it's bewilderment over how to deal with all those veg leftovers. You know, the unglamorous knobbly roots of shame, that tend to get shunted to the back of the fridge for days on end. After all, there are only so many bowls of vegetable soup one can stomach before tedium sets in.

It's a good idea to check out your nearest markets and ethnic shops for vegetables. Don't be afraid to experiment with the different varieties of spinach, gourd, squash and beans on offer, give things a prod and have a good old haggle. It might appear a bit alien at first, but once you familiarise yourself, it's easy to work out that most things fall into the rough subheadings of pulse, leaf, root and fruit.

As well as being easier on the purse and the planet, vegetarian meals tend to be healthier. Not in a sanctimonious, 'rainbow rhythms' way, but also in the vainest of manners imaginable. Meat-shirkers tend to boast healthier skin, hair, nails, weight and breath, for the simple reason that most of them are getting their five a day and then some.

There's so much possibility with a bag of veg, it definitely pushes your cooking to more creative places, in ways that a bloody lump of swine just doesn't. In short, you won't find any cheese omelettes in this chapter. What you will come across are the kind of recipes that'll have your meat and two veg pals oblivious to the lack of dead animal on their plate, and demanding third helpings every time.

ROOT VEGETABLE RÖSTI

tuck in!

A cracking way of ploughing through all those vegetables you tend to get overloaded with once root season is fully upon us. I like to add raw beetroot and parsnips for colour and sweetness, but grate in whatever you've got. It's especially satisfying to feed this to people who claim not to like vegetables, just to witness them swoonfully chow down their words. Splendiferous with a fried egg and a blob of brown sauce, it's an awesome little number for Sunday brunch if you're feeding a crowd.

Serves 4

2 large waxy potatoes
2 carrots
4 beetroot
½ small celeriac
2 parsnips
8–10 Brussels sprouts
1 tablespoon rice bran or olive oil

50g butter
1 onion, diced
1 tablespoon finely chopped fresh dill
1 tablespoon finely chopped fresh parsley
8 fresh sage leaves, finely chopped
1 teaspoon dried mixed herbs
salt and freshly ground black pepper
4 eggs

Peel and grate the potatoes, carrots, beetroot, celeriac, parsnips and Brussels sprouts. This is obviously a thousand times easier if you have a food processor with a grating attachment, otherwise, just stick something on the iPlayer, get out the box grater and think of how much upper arm definition you're building and the cash you're saving on gym membership.

Try to remove as much moisture as possible from the veg by squeezing in a clean tea towel lined with kitchen paper and then emptying onto a baking sheet and placing in a low oven (150°C/gas mark 2) for 10–15 minutes.

Glug the oil into a 35cm, non-stick, heavy-based frying pan. Add half the butter and gently sweat the onion for 20 minutes.

Stir the fresh and dried herbs into the shredded vegetable mixture and season well with salt and pepper. Mix thoroughly. Add enough of the vegetable mix to line the pan without over filling it. (Any mixture that won't fit can be frozen for another time.) Dot over the remaining butter and cook over a low heat for 20 minutes or until dry and caramelised underneath. Carefully flip the rösti over, sprinkle with more salt if necessary, and cook the other side for 20 minutes. When crisp and cooked throughout, keep warm in the oven.

Add a little more butter or oil to the pan you used for the rösti and fry the eggs. Slice the rösti into wedges and serve immediately with the eggs on top.

CHICKPEA & CELERIAC PANCAKES

with toasted feta & avocado salsa

One of those brilliant dishes that's redolent of Wow and Ooh la la! And nothing whatsoever like health food (but secretly very, very good for you). The layers of flavour and textures are a top way of making a feature of the vegetables, rather than attempting to conceal them, as so many vegetarian dishes are prone to do. I have a bit of a cumin addiction, so like to whack in 2 teaspoons, but you can always add less and up the chilli or mustard seed quotient instead, if you prefer.

Serves 2

For the topping
100g feta cheese
olive oil, to drizzle and for frying
1 large avocado, chopped
6 small vine tomatoes, chopped
1½ tablespoons chopped fresh
   coriander leaves

1 spring onion, finely chopped
salt
1 dessertspoon chives, finely chopped
1 very small garlic clove, crushed
juice of ½ lemon

Preheat the grill to medium.

Place the feta cheese in one piece, in a heatproof, shallow dish and drizzle with a little olive oil. Brown under the grill for 15–18 minutes or until wobbly and tanned.

Mash the remaining topping ingredients, except the butter and sunflower seeds, together in a bowl. Crumble in the feta. Set aside.

For the pancakes
650g peeled celeriac, scrubbed and grated
1 red onion, finely diced
85g chickpea (gram) flour
1 green chilli, finely chopped
2 teaspoons cumin seeds

1 teaspoon mustard seeds
1 teaspoon salt
1 teaspoon baking powder
knob of butter
1 large egg
1 tablespoon toasted sunflower seeds

Mix the grated celeriac, red onion, chickpea flour, chilli, cumin, mustard, salt and baking powder for about 5 minutes to allow everything to combine and swell a little. Crack in the egg and stir well to form a rich batter.

Heat a small omelette pan and add a slick of oil and the butter. Fry the pancakes, two tablespoonfuls of mixture at a time for about 5 minutes on each side. While the remainder are cooking, keep the pancakes warm in a low oven (150°C/gas mark 2). Serve with lashings of the feta avocado mix and a sprinkling of toasted sunflower seeds.

DOUBLE LENTIL DOUGHNUTS
in roasted cumin and tamarind yogurt

This Indian classic is one I've been making since just about forever. You can buy ginormous bags of urad lentils from ethnic shops or online. The doughnuts need a good soak in the spiced yogurt, so don't stress about keeping them crisp, as they're meant to be meltingly soft. This is at its zenith a couple of hours after a prolonged session in the fridge, when the flavours have intertwined and blossomed. Gorgeous with a simple bowl of dhal and roti or as a cooling accompaniment to my Chickpea and Tomato Curry (see page 31).

Makes 10-12

160g urad dhal (white) lentils, soaked in cold water for 2 hours
90g yellow split lentils, soaked in cold water for 2 hours
1 tablespoon grated fresh root ginger
1 garlic clove, crushed
2 green chillies, finely chopped
salt
vegetable oil, for deep frying

1–2 teaspoons cumin seeds
500g Greek yogurt
4 medium tomatoes, diced
½ cucumber, diced
3 spring onions, finely chopped
1 tablespoon finely chopped fresh coriander leaves, plus extra to serve
1 teaspoon chilli powder
1–2 teaspoons salt
chilli powder and tamarind sauce, to serve

Drain the lentils and place in a food processor with the ginger, garlic and chillies, season with salt and blitz to a nice thick, cement-sludge of a paste.

Preheat the oil in a large saucepan or wok and have a large bowl of warm tap water ready and a couple of plates lined with kitchen paper.

Place a square of clingfilm on your palm and spoon on a tablespoon of the mixture. Shape into a doughnut shape by teasing out the centre of the blobs with a teaspoon. Gently slide into the hot oil. Repeat to add 2 more doughnuts to the pan. Drain the doughnuts on the kitchen paper and then drop into the warm water for about 30 seconds. Drain and gently squeeze the water from the doughnuts and set aside. Repeat this process until all the mixture has been cooked (10–12 doughnuts in total).

Toast the cumin seeds in a hot, non-stick, dry frying pan until fragrant. Grind the toasted seeds to a powder, using a pestle and mortar.

Mix the yogurt with the tomatoes, cucumber, spring onion and coriander. Stir in the ground cumin, salt and chilli powder. Pour the yogurt mixture over the doughnuts, sprinkle with the coriander and a little more chilli powder and zig zag over the tamarind sauce to serve.

LENTIL AND LEEK FRITTERS
with a tomato, soured cream and carom dressing

These feisty little bites are a great starter and also make a nice, crunchy accompaniment to my Creamy Beetroot and Black Lentil Dahl (see page 102). Carom seeds (also known as ajwain) are very fragrant, they look like smaller, paler version of cumin seeds and have a prounounced thyme-like flavour. Try to use the absolute minimum of water when blending the pulses. It's all about keeping those textures intact!

Serves 4

For the dressing
3 tablespoons soured cream
4 tablespoons Greek yogurt
½ teaspoon dried mint or dill
½ teaspoon carom seeds
1 tablespoon finely chopped fresh parsley
5 medium tomatoes, chopped
½ teaspoon salt

Combine all the dressing ingredients in a bowl and stir well. Set aside to chill.

For the fritters
100g red lentils, soaked in cold water for
    1 hour
2 onions, halved and very finely sliced
1 leek, halved and very finely sliced
35g fresh root ginger, grated
4 garlic cloves, crushed
2 green chillies, finely sliced
1 tablespoon finely chopped fresh coriander
½ teaspoon turmeric
1 teaspoon ground cumin
1 teaspoon chilli powder
¼ teaspoon baking powder
½ teaspoon salt
50g rice flour
vegetable oil, for deep frying
warmed pitta bread, to serve

Drain the lentils and blitz for 2–3 minutes in a food processor until smooth.

Combine the onions, leek, ginger, garlic, fresh chilli and coriander in a bowl. Add the turmeric, cumin, chilli powder, baking powder and salt and mix well. Finally stir in the blitzed lentils. Add the flour and stir until very thick.

Heat the oil to about 190°C in a wok and drop dessertspoonfuls of the mixture in batches of 4–6 into the hot oil, taking care not to overcrowd. Fry until dark brown and crunchy, about 5–10 minutes. Drain on plenty of kitchen paper. Repeat until all the mixture is used up.

Stuff the fritters into hot pitta pockets and smother with the creamy dressing.

If you have any leftover, these make a smart lunch in a wrap with some salad and cheese.

CHIPOTLE BEAN QUESADILLAS

with tomato & doughnut peach salsa

Dead easy to make and jaw-droppingly tasty, you'll find yourself turning to these time and again. It's a good idea to stock up on tortillas and can of chilli beans just in case you get the urge. Use nectarines or standard peaches in the salsa if you can't find doughnut ones. If you really want to stick it to Old Father Time, you can always make the salsa and the guacamole in advance. A grade 'A' certified crowd pleaser if ever there was one.

Serves 4

For the guacamole
2 ripe avocados
juice of 1 lime
1 garlic clove, crushed
1 spring onion, finely chopped
1 chilli, finely chopped
1 teaspoon salt
handful of roughly chopped fresh coriander

Mash the avocados and squeeze in the lime juice. Add the crushed garlic, spring onion, chilli, salt and the coriander and blend well. Set aside.

For the salsa
1 teaspoon cumin seeds
2 doughnut peaches, destoned and diced
4 medium vine tomatoes, diced
1 tablespoon rice or cider vinegar
½ tablespoon mustard or olive oil
2 tablespoons finely chopped fresh coriander
large pinch of salt
1 teaspoon sugar
2 spring onions or 1 red onion, finely chopped
½ garlic clove, crushed
1 green chilli, finely chopped

Toast the cumin seeds in a hot, non-stick, dry frying pan until fragrant. Grind the toasted seeds to a powder, using a pestle and mortar.

Make the tomato and peach salsa by crushing the peaches and tomatoes together and adding the ground cumin, vinegar, mustard or olive oil, chopped coriander, large pinch of salt, sugar, spring onion, garlic and chilli. Stir well and set aside.

For the quesadillas
2 x 290g cans mixed beans in chilli sauce
1½ teaspoons ground cumin
1 teaspoon dried oregano
1 teaspoon dried chilli flakes
2 teaspoons chipotle paste
oil, for frying
12 corn tortillas
Cheddar cheese, grated
soured cream and finely chopped fresh
    coriander, to serve

Heat the beans in a small pan for 15 minutes. Stir in the cumin, oregano, dried chilli flakes and chipotle paste. In a frying pan, heat a slick of oil. Fry 1 tortilla and smear in a spoonful of beans over half of the tortilla. Add a dollop of guacamole and sprinkle over some of the cheese. Fold over the second half of the tortilla and gently press the edges together to seal. Flip over and brown on the other side. Repeat to cook and fill the remaining tortillas. Serve with a liberal spoonful of the fruity salsa, the soured cream and a sprinkle of finely chopped coriander.

MARINATED HALLOUMI, PALM HEART & SPINACH SALAD

with passion fruit dressing

I've got a terrible soft spot for the squeaky brown wonder that is cooked halloumi and find that marinating with garlic, chilli and lime makes it doubly moreish. This is pure escapism via the medium of salad: the passion fruit dressing adds a blast of technicolour verve and the hearts of palm are just the final touch to transport you somewhere tropical and altogether more exotic.

Serves 2

For the dressing
3 or 4 passion fruit
juice of ½ lime
2 tablespoons clear honey
1 tablespoon avocado or walnut oil
1 tablespoon rice vinegar
1 teaspoon soy sauce

Scoop the pulp and seeds out of the passion fruit, if you're not keen on the seeds, gently heat the pulp and seeds, cool and strain, then discard the seeds. Mix the dressing ingredients and taste – it should be sweet, sharp, sour and salty. Set aside.

For the salad
250g halloumi cheese, cubed
1 garlic clove, finely chopped
juice of 1 lime
1 red chilli, finely chopped
100g brown basmati rice
250ml vegetable stock
2 big handfuls of spinach
1 mango, diced
410g can palm hearts, drained and cut
   into chunks
1 carrot, shredded
2 tablespoons chopped fresh coriander
2 tablespoons chopped fresh mint leaves
1 tablespoon each of sunflower, pumpkin and
   sesame seeds, toasted

Place the cubed halloumi in a non-metallic shallow container, add the garlic, lime juice and chilli and set aside to marinade.

Boil the rice in the stock for 30 minutes, uncovered. Stir in the spinach and steam for 5 minutes with the lid on to wilt. Transfer to a serving dish and set aside to cool.

In a small frying pan, fry the halloumi, for 5 minutes, until golden all over.

Stir the cheese, mango, palm hearts, carrot and herbs into the cooled rice and serve with the seeds and dressing sprinkled over.

CREAMY BEETROOT & BLACK LENTIL DHAL

Makhani dhal is my go-to pulse-based comfort dish of choice. It's a great example of how Punjabis know best when it comes to hearty fare. Here I've added beetroot to echo the earthy, mineral savour, not to mention add a vibrant magenta pop, which makes a nice change from the usual sludgy brown. Creamy yet healthy, this is ace with hot chapatis and a whirl of yogurt.

Serves 6-8

For the dhal
150g black lentils/whole urad dhal,
    soaked in cold water overnight
150g dried red kidney beans, soaked in cold
    water overnight
50g yellow split peas/chana dal, soaked
    in cold water overnight

250g beetroot, grated
500ml vegetable or chicken stock
3-4 garlic cloves, crushed
2 green chillies, finely chopped
35g fresh root ginger, chopped
1 onion, quartered
1 cinnamon stick
1 teaspoon turmeric

Drain the lentils and kidney beans, wash thoroughly and place in a large pan. Add the beetroot, stock, garlic, chillies, ginger, onion, cinnamon and turmeric to the pan and cook for 40 minutes–1 hour or until the lentils and beans are tender, adding a little water if it starts to dry out.

To temper
50g butter or ghee
1 teaspoon cumin
½ teaspoons fenugreek seeds

2 garlic cloves, sliced
a pinch of asafoetida (optional)
400g can chopped tomatoes
1-2 teaspoons salt

Melt the butter in a frying pan and add the cumin and fenugreek seeds, once they pop add the garlic slices and fry until golden. Add the asafoetida, tomatoes and salt before stirring into the dhal.

To finish
1 teaspoon chilli powder
100g butter

2 tablespoons double cream or Greek yogurt
½ teaspoons garam masala
hot chapatis and natural yogurt, to serve

Mash the lentils slightly and reheat, adding the chilli powder, butter and cream or yogurt. Simmer for 30 minutes and stir in the garam masala.

Check and adjust the seasoning before serving with hot chapatis and a dollop of natural yogurt.

WINTER GREENS IN ROSEMARY, ONION & PARMESAN SAUCE

This gratin is a pretty unctuous way to obliterate any yawnsome old greens that might be skulking at the back of the salad drawer. A nice, simple supper for two, the infused milk really elevates this dish from a mere cheese sauce; so try to get that flavour going overnight if you can.

Serves 2

1 onion
6 cloves
1 bay leaf
8 black peppercorns
3–4 sprigs fresh rosemary
600ml whole milk
25g butter
1 tablespoon plain flour

190g Parmesan cheese, grated
salt and freshly ground black pepper
500g combination of any of the following:
    kale, roughly chopped; broccoli, divided into
    florets; Brussels sprouts, de-stemmed
    and quartered
50g hazelnuts or pine nuts, toasted and
    roughly chopped
baguette, to serve

The night before (or at least 2 hours in advance) stud the onion with the cloves and pop it with the bay leaf, peppercorns and sprigs of rosemary in a jug with the milk and leave the flavours to work their magic.

Melt the butter in a small non-stick saucepan, stir in the flour and cook over a low heat for 5 minutes, stirring well. Strain the flavoured milk gradually into the flour and butter paste, stirring all the time. Add 150g of the cheese, and stir until melted. Season with salt and pepper.

If you are using kale and/or Brussels sprouts, cook them in boiling water for 5 minutes.

Preheat the oven to 200°C/gas mark 6. Arrange the greens in a 1.5 litre casserole dish and mix well with the hazelnuts or pine nuts. Pour over the sauce and sprinkle with the remaining cheese.

Bake for 30 minutes or until golden and bubbling. Serve with plenty of ripped up warm baguette to mop up the sauce.

LUXURY MUSHROOM & BRAZIL NUT WELLINGTONS

with sage & onion filling

So much more than a nut roast. Taking the choicest elements of a traditional Sunday roast, like sage and onion and parsnips, and creating something with truckloads of depth, makes for a bullet train straight to deliciousville.

Serves 6-8

For the filling
1 tablespoon butter
2 onions, finely chopped
1 teaspoon sugar
2 tablespoons finely chopped fresh
    sage leaves (reserve the stems)

pinch of salt
75g strong hard cheese, grated e.g. Cheddar
1 teaspoon balsamic vinegar
1 tablespoon cream cheese
freshly ground black pepper

Melt the butter in a pan. Add the onions, sugar, half the sage stems and a little salt. Caramelise the onions over a very low heat for about 30 minutes. Cool, and discard the sage stems. Combine the rest of the filling ingredients in a bowl, season with pepper and stir into the onions.

For the wellingtons
1 tablespoon olive oil
1 red onion, finely chopped
3 garlic cloves, crushed
2 bay leaves
250g mushrooms, chopped
1 parsnip, diced
2 tablespoons chopped fresh parsley
2 tablespoons chopped fresh thyme
2 tablespoons chopped fresh rosemary
½ teaspoon smoked paprika

pinch of dried oregano
juice of ½ lemon
2–3 teaspoons Worcestershire sauce
250ml red wine
500ml vegetable stock
80g oatcakes
150g mixed nuts
salt and freshly ground black pepper
butter, for greasing
flour, for dusting
375g ready rolled all-butter puff pastry
1 egg, beaten

Heat the olive oil in a large pan and sweat the red onion, garlic, bay leaves and remaining sage stems for 5 minutes until the onion is soft. Add the mushrooms, parsnip, parsley, thyme, rosemary, paprika, oregano, lemon juice and Worcestershire sauce. Stir well, turn up the heat and cook for about 20 minutes. Slosh in the wine and reduce for 4-5 minutes, until almost evaporated. Add the stock and cook on a high heat for 15–20 minutes (until the parsnip is tender and the liquid has reduced to a couple of syrupy tablespoons). Set aside to cool.

Process the oatcakes in a food processor. Add the nuts and continue to blitz. Scrape in the cooled mushroom mixture and process. Adjust the seasoning if necessary.

Preheat the oven to 180°C/gas mark 4. Line a baking tray with greased and floured baking parchment. On a lightly floured surface roll out the pastry to 35 x 25cm and place on the lined tray. Spoon half the sage and onion mixture down the middle. Spoon the filling on top of this. Top with the remaining sage mix and make a lattice by slashing the pastry on either side of the filling into 3cm strips. Brush the pastry with egg on the inside and fold over the top of the filling. Brush the outside with plenty of egg too and bake for around 40 minutes or until golden.

POACHED MUSHROOM PUY LENTIL
& cheesy leek shepherd's pie

Another spectacular way to transform your humble veg into suppertime A listers. Even the most die hard carnivorous types will barely register the lack of any meat.

Serves 6-8

For the mushrooms
450g mushrooms, roughly chopped
250ml red wine
2 bay leaves

600ml vegetable stock
2 garlic cloves, crushed
2 teaspoons dried thyme
1 small bunch fresh parsley
2 tablespoons tomato ketchup
2 tablespoons Worcestershire sauce

Place the mushrooms, red wine, bay leaves, half the vegetable stock, garlic, thyme and parsley in a saucepan for 2–3 hours or overnight. Bring the pan of mushrooms to the boil and simmer gently, uncovered for 20 minutes, until the sauce thickens slightly. Remove from the heat and drain the mushrooms, reserving the marinating liquid. Discard the parsley and bay leaves. Preheat the grill to medium-high. Mix the ketchup and Worcestershire sauce together. Brush the mushrooms liberally with the mixture, and grill for 10 minutes or so until nicely caramelised.

For the lentils and vegetables
150g puy lentils
40g butter
1 tablespoon oil
1 medium onion, finely chopped
3 garlic cloves, finely chopped
300g carrots, diced

340g parsnips, diced
½ teaspoon paprika
1–2 sprigs fresh rosemary, leaves
    picked and chopped
salt and freshly ground black pepper
2 Parmesan cheese rinds

Place the lentils in a pan with the remaining stock and simmer gently for 25-30 minutes or until tender. In a medium saucepan, melt the butter and oil and add the onion and garlic, and cook for 15 minutes. Once these have softened add the carrots, parsnips, paprika, rosemary and salt and pepper. Cook for 15 minutes or until golden. Stir in the lentils, cheese rinds and the mushroom marinating liquid. Turn the heat up and cook for 5-10 minutes until most of the liquid has evaporated, with only a little sauce remaining. Remove the cheese rinds, season and set aside.

For the topping
750g potatoes, roughly chopped
300g celeriac, roughly chopped
150ml whole milk
40g butter
freshly grated nutmeg, to season

salt and freshly ground black pepper
1 tablespoon olive oil
2 leeks, thinly sliced
75g strong Gouda, grated
75g Parmesan or Cheddar cheese, grated

Cook the potatoes and celeriac in a pan of boiling salted water for 15–20 minutes or until tender. Drain. Add the milk, butter and nutmeg, season and mash. Heat the oil in a frying pan and cook the leeks for 5 minutes until soft. Preheat the oven to 180°C/gas mark 4. Spread the lentils and vegetables in a large, deep ovenproof dish. Arrange the mushrooms on top. Spread the mashed potato and celeriac over. Sprinkle with the leeks and cheese. Bake the pie for 30–40 minutes.

SMOKED AUBERGINE, SPINACH PESTO
& red pepper lasagne

Turtelly and utterly bellissimo. This only needs a snappy green salad and crusty bread to mop up the delicious juices.

Serves 4-6

For the roasted pepper and red wine sauce
3 red peppers
1 tablespoon olive oil
2 small onions, finely chopped
2 garlic cloves, finely chopped

2 tablespoons tomato purée
200ml red wine
400g can chopped tomatoes
1–2 tablespoons torn fresh basil leaves
pinch of sugar
salt and freshly ground black pepper

Preheat the oven to 200°C/gas mark 6. Roast the peppers for 30 minutes until soft and slightly charred. Leave to cool in a plastic bag. Heat the olive oil in a pan and soften the onion and garlic for 8–10 minutes. Stir in the tomato purée and red wine. Turn the heat up to reduce by two thirds. Pour in the chopped tomatoes, fresh basil and sugar and season. Simmer for 10–15 minutes.

For the smoked aubergine bechamel sauce
2 small/medium aubergines
50g butter
2 tablespoons plain flour

500ml whole milk
75g Parmesan cheese, grated
salt and freshly ground black pepper

Flame roast the aubergines (they also blister well on an electric hob so don't stress if you don't have gas) until blackened all over and collapsed. Peel and then mash the flesh until it's like a purée and set aside. Melt the butter in a small non-stick saucepan and stir in the flour. Cook the flour paste for at least 5 minutes, until the mixture is pale brown. Gradually stir in the milk and melt in the Parmesan. Stir in the aubergine and season with salt and pepper.

For the spinach pesto
1 tablespoon olive oil
2 heaped tablespoon pine nuts
1 clove garlic, crushed

500g spinach leaves
500g lasagne sheets
2 tablespoons fresh basil leaves
125g mozzarella cheese, sliced

Heat the olive oil in a frying pan, toast the pine nuts and add the garlic and cook gently until everything is golden and fragrant. Turn the heat down and add in a few handfuls of spinach, place a lid on and allow it to wilt a little before adding more. When it's all wilted, turn off the heat, allow to cool, squeeze out any excess liquid and roughly chop.

Peel and roughly chop the roasted peppers and add to the tomato sauce. Blitz the sauce with a hand-held electric blender until smooth. It should be fairly thick so continue to reduce it until you're happy with the consistency.

To assemble, layer one third of the spinach on the bottom of a 23 x 23 x 5cm dish, pour over one third of the pepper sauce. Top with lasagne sheets and drizzle over one third of the aubergine bechamel sauce. Top with a few torn basil leaves. Repeat the layers twice more, (make sure you leave a decent sized gap at the top of your dish as the lasagne sheets will expand) and scatter over the mozzarella. Bake for 45 minutes until it's bubblicious and tanned to perfection.

HEALTH KICK MUFFINS

mmm!

These are interplanetary light years away from those over-sugary, oversized shop-bought monstrosities. They last for a week and are an absolute doddle to make. There are no hard and fast rules, so use any fruit and nuts you happen to have to hand (dried blueberries, cherries, brazils or cashews all work well). A super simple and tasty way of pumping some goodness into your system on the sly, without it even realising.

Makes 12

Dry ingredients
50g walnuts, pecans or hazelnuts
100g prunes or dried apricots
200g self-raising wholemeal flour
50g linseeds or linseed powder
50g wheatgerm
50g porridge oats
3 teaspoons baking powder
¼ teaspoon mixed spice
½ teaspoon ground cinnamon
100g sultanas
50g light muscovado sugar

Preheat the oven to 190°C/gas mark 5. Place 12 paper muffin cases on 2 baking trays or in muffin trays.

Place all the dry ingredients in a large bowl and stir well to combine.

Wet ingredients
100ml olive or coconut oil
150g natural yogurt
150ml milk
1 egg, beaten
1 teaspoon vanilla extract
2 bananas, mashed
2 apples, grated
1 large carrot, grated

Add all the wet ingredients and mix thoroughly.

Divide the mixture equally between the muffin cases. Bake for about 20-30 minutes – they are done when a clean, inserted skewer comes out dry.

Transfer to a wire rack to cool. Store in an airtight container for up to 1 week.

MATCHA ROLY POLY PUDDING

with greengage jam & stem ginger custard

Roly poly pudding is one of those quietly brilliant dishes that we should all be more proud of. Here I've made an Oriental version, with Matcha (powdered green tea), greengage jam and stem ginger custard, to levitate it from the drudgery of school dinners. You can buy greengage jam from most supermarkets, but just use whatever jam you have to hand.

Serves 6-8

For the stem ginger custard
300ml whole milk
250ml double cream
1 vanilla pod
4 egg yolks

2 tablespoons caster sugar
2 tablespoons cornflour
2 tablespoons stem ginger syrup
5 nuggets of stem ginger in syrup, drained
    and chopped
butter, for dotting

First make the custard. Pour the milk and cream into a small pan, scrape the seeds from the vanilla pod, and put the seeds and pod in the pan too. Gently heat to just below boiling point.

Meanwhile, place the yolks, sugar and cornflour in a little bowl and whisk well. Gradually introduce the yolk mixture to the hot creamy milk, one spoonful at a time. Whisk continuously over a low heat for about 5–10 minutes, until a thick custard forms. Remove the vanilla pod, add the ginger syrup and chopped stem ginger and dot with a little butter and remove from the heat. Cover with clingfilm.

For the Matcha roly poly
400g plain flour, plus extra for dusting
50g butter, cubed
80g vegetable suet
100g caster sugar
2 teaspoons baking powder
1 tablespoon Matcha

1 teaspoon ground mace or freshly
    grated nutmeg
1 medium egg
100ml whole milk
100ml double cream
300g greengage jam

To make the pudding, place the flour and butter in a large mixing bowl and rub them together to form breadcrumbs. Stir in the suet and add the sugar, baking powder, Matcha and mace or nutmeg. Beat the egg, milk and cream together and gradually add to the flour until you're left with a stiff-ish dough.

Preheat the oven to 170°C/gas mark 3. Cut a piece of baking parchment to fit in the bottom of a large roasting tin. Place the paper on the work surface, sprinkle with a little flour and pat the dough out on it to form a rectangle roughly 40 x 30cm. Smother half of the jam over this, then roll up, starting at the shorter end, into a Swiss roll shape using the paper and a spatula to ease matters along.

Lift the paper and dough into the dish and bake for 1½ hours – it should be cracked on top but still nice and moist within. Spread the remaining jam over the warm pudding. Reheat the stem ginger custard and spoon generously over the roly poly pudding to serve.

PORTABLE FEASTS

Stuffing your face in the sunshine, surely it's what summers were made for? What can beat a spot of al fresco dining when the weather's all scorchio and your appetite's well and truly fired up? If you want to bypass that wilting old supermarket sub of disappointment, then look no further. With a little forward thinking, you could be clicking open your plastic tub of dreams to an absolute vision of smoked potato salad or some extremely tasty roast chicken pies of distinction. You know, the sort of thing that makes lunchtime the technicolour hour in a thoroughly black and white kind of day. There's not even any need to bust a gut especially – mine are all dishes you could make for supper the night before, and then slip any leftovers for the next day into an old takeaway box.

If you do decide to brave a portable feast in the great outdoors, then there are factors other than those of the UVA/B variety that need to be accounted for. Now is not the time for finickity salads or soggy sandwiches. Instead, pack a hunk of melon, a few whole tomatoes and salad leaves, a jam jar of dressing and a small knife to hack everything up with on site. If it's properly sweltersville outside, stick a couple of water or juice bottles in the freezer before heading out (these will double up as chill blocks as they defrost en route). If you're taking cheese, go for Brie or Camembert, which are both partial to a spot of melty weather, and leave the Cheddar at home, it'll only go greasy. Finally, don't forget to take plenty of facial wipes, plus a spare carrier bag for any post-picnic rubbish. Oh, and a brolly, of course.

LUNCH TIME!

I wonder what sandwich-chain soup is on today? Might treat myself to a soggy sarnie with more calories in it than a dirty burger. Do you want me to pick you up an overpriced coffee while I'm out?

AAAARRRRGGH!

It's unbelievable how much people will spend in those places every month!

It doesn't take that much time to cook a pan of rice and roast some veggies.

That's a gourmet rice salad for a fraction of the price and no endless picking out the green peppers.

Come on, you're at work! You need something to make the day exciting!

FETA, DILL & BEETROOT SAVOURY CHEESECAKE

say cheese!

This savoury cheesecake is one of those dishes that's so good, it's easy to forget there's no meat involved. The tastebuds are too busy honing in on how well the Parmesan base, horseradish-flecked beetroot and the smooth, herbal feta topping just bleed and meld into fresh, creamy mouthfuls of bliss. Make mini ones for a sophisticated starter or serve with the Nectarine and tomato gazpacho (see page 155), a big verdant salad and a fancy protein platter in the height of summer for maximum impact. Acid pink and white, it's beautiful to look at and makes for a stunner of a centrepiece.

Serves 6-8

For the base
butter, for greasing
65g white dried breadcrumbs
50g Parmesan cheese, grated
1 teaspoon black onion seeds or nigella seeds
freshly ground black pepper
50g butter, melted

Preheat the oven to 170°C/gas mark 3. Grease and line a 20cm loose-bottomed cake tin with baking parchment.

Make the base by mixing together the breadcrumbs, Parmesan and onion or nigella seeds, season with black pepper and pour in the melted butter and mix well. It should be a little claggy at this stage. Press into the prepared tin and bake for 15 minutes. Set aside to cool.

For the topping
200g feta cheese
180g curd cheese
120g single cream
2 tablespoons chopped fresh chives
4 tablespoons chopped fresh dill
4 spring onions, white part only,
   finely chopped
220g beetroot, grated
1 tablespoon creamed horseradish
2 large egg whites
juice of ½ lemon
10g sachet vegetarian gelatine substitute

Mash the feta in a mixing bowl, add the curd cheese, single cream, chives and half of the dill and beat together.

In another bowl, mix the spring onion into the beetroot and mix well with the horseradish. Spoon this onto the cheesecake base and spread it out evenly with the back of a spoon.

Whisk the egg whites to the soft peak stage. Place the lemon juice and 3 tablespoons of cold water in a small pan, sprinkle the vegetarian gelatine over and turn up the heat until it reaches boiling point. Beat this quickly into the cheesy cream mixture and gently fold in the egg whites, 1 tablespoonful at a time. Layer this over the top of the beetroot mixture and cover with clingfilm. Refrigerate overnight.

Garnish with the remaining dill and serve.

SMOKED CHEDDAR, BALSAMIC SPRING ONION
& nigella seed quiche

Quiche should ideally be made the day before you want to eat it, to give it time to set and allow the flavours to develop properly. I've been slipping nigella seeds into my savoury cheese-based dishes for years – the oniony twist is a key ingredient in so many Bengali dishes. Here it magically spruces up a cheese and onion quiche, while the seam of balsamic spring onion adds a tangy dimension. All in all, the whole thing makes for a bit of a textural disco in your mouth.

Serves 4-6

80g butter, plus extra for greasing
160g plain flour, plus extra for dusting
2 teaspoons nigella seeds
2 tablespoons balsamic vinegar
1 tablespoon clear honey

1 bunch spring onions
4 eggs, beaten
100ml double cream
175g smoked Cheddar cheese, grated
1 tablespoon finely chopped fresh parsley
salt and freshly ground black pepper

Preheat the oven to 200°C/gas mark 6. Grease and line a 24cm quiche tin with baking parchment.

Rub the butter, flour and nigella seeds lightly together until they resemble breadcrumbs. Add 2-3 tablespoons cold water and stir to form a soft dough. Wrap and chill in the fridge for 15-20 minutes. Roll out the pastry on a floured surface and line the prepared tin with the pastry. Cover the pastry with baking parchment and baking beans or lentils and bake blind for 15 minutes. Remove the paper and beans and cook for a further 5 minutes. Remove from the oven and set aside to cool. Reduce the oven temperature to 170°C/gas mark 3.

Preheat the grill to high. Line a grill pan with foil. Mix the balsamic vinegar with the honey. Place the whole spring onions on the lined pan and pour the honeyed vinegar mixture over. Grill for 5-7 minutes or until the onions are soft and blistered in places. Set aside to cool and then finely chop.

Beat the eggs and cream together in a large jug and mix in the cheese and parsley. Season with salt and pepper. Place the pastry case on a baking sheet. Line the quiche with the balsamic spring onions and pour over the cream and cheese mixture. Bake for about 20 minutes or until set and golden.

ROASTED WOODSMOKE BBQ CHICKPEAS

Roasting chickpeas adds a real nutty depth charge of flavour, and doing so with BBQ sauce, garlic and olive oil equates to a healthy snack with a hefty moreish factor. Making these is the definition of simplicity. You can of course, always use a drained can of chickpeas, but the dried, soaked and boiled ones are just so, so good.

Serves 2-4

200g dried chickpeas, soaked in cold
   water overnight
1 tablespoon woodsmoke BBQ brown sauce

1 fat garlic clove, finely grated or crushed
1 teaspoon salt
1 tablespoon olive oil

Preheat the oven to 200°C/gas mark 6. Line a roasting tray with baking parchment.

Drain the soaked chickpeas, cover in fresh water and boil for 1 hour. Dry the chickpeas well in a tea towel.

Combine the BBQ sauce with the garlic, salt and olive oil in a large bowl. Toss in the chickpeas, mixing well.

Pour the chickpeas into the roasting tin in a single layer. Roast for about 20 minutes, or until brown and crisp.

ROASTED PUMPKIN QUINOA SALAD

with hazelnut pesto

Bleurrgh. I absolutely loathe quinoa. But like most people, I have a box of the wretched stuff skulking about at the back of the cupboard, hidden away behind the Arborio and purchased in a hungover pique of health kick guilt. But fear not, the uninspiring taste can be masked. This gutsy pesto is also really tasty stirred into a simple coleslaw of cabbage, red onion and carrots.

Serves 2

For the salad
½ squash or ¼ pumpkin, hacked into wedges
1 tablespoon chilli oil

1 teaspoon sea salt
1 teaspoon fresh chopped rosemary
70g quinoa
150ml vegetable stock

Preheat the oven to 180°C/gas mark 2.

Sprinkle the squash or pumpkin with chilli oil, salt and rosemary and transfer to a roasting tin. Roast for 40 minutes or until tender.

Place the quinoa and stock in a saucepan and cook according to the pack instructions. Set aside to cool.

For the pesto
80g hazelnuts
1 teaspoon cumin seeds
4 tablespoons avocado oil or extra
    virgin olive oil
juice of ½ lemon

1 fat garlic clove, crushed
2 tablespoons finely chopped sage leaves
½ teaspoon salt
65g vintage Gruyère, Gouda or Old
    Amsterdam cheese, grated

Toast the hazelnuts in a hot, non-stick, dry frying pan until golden and fragrant. Transfer to a food processor. Toast the cumin seeds in the same frying pan until golden and fragrant and add to the food processor. Add the oil, lemon juice, garlic, sage, salt and cheese to the food processor and blend until smooth.

Combine well with the quinoa and the squash or pumpkin.

ADUKI BEAN FALAFELS
with miso garlic tahini

Adukis tend to be one of the more overlooked pulses, yet each tiny red powerhouse of a bean is saturated with goodness. Prized all over Asia for their nutritional qualities, they cook up magically in falafel and add a pleasing textural layer. The miso garlic tahini is the perfect thing to drench them in. Cocooned in a wrap or served with lots of crudités they make for the finest picnic fodder.

Makes 18

For the miso garlic tahini
1 very small garlic clove
1 teaspoon salt
4 tablespoons Greek yogurt
2 dessertspoons tahini
2 teaspoons red miso paste

Using a pestle and mortar, crush the garlic and salt together to form a paste. Combine the remaining miso garlic tahini ingredients with the paste in a small bowl. Set aside.

For the falafels
100g dried aduki beans, soaked in cold
  water overnight
100g dried butter beans, soaked in cold
  water overnight
1 teaspoon ground cumin
1 teaspoon salt
2 garlic cloves, crushed
¼ teaspoon baking powder
2 tablespoons plain flour
1 onion, finely chopped
3 tablespoons each of finely chopped fresh
  parsley and coriander
oil, for deep frying
salad, pickled chillies and flatbread, to serve

Drain the butter beans and aduki beans and simmer in fresh water for 1 hour.

Drain the cooked beans and blitz in a food processor with the cumin, salt, garlic, baking powder and flour (don't worry if they don't all blend to a uniform purée, it's nice to have some whole bits for texture). It should be mushy enough to form firm spheres, so add a tablespoon or two of flour if it looks too wet. Stir the finely chopped onion, the parsley and the coriander in (don't process this as you'll end up diluting the flavour of the onion). Shape the mixture into 18 little balls and place on greaseproof paper until you are ready to cook.

Heat the oil in a wok or deep fryer to 190°C and fry the falafels in batches of 6, for 4–5 minutes or until they are a deep brown colour, to ensure a half decent crunch. Drain on kitchen paper and cook the remaining falafels.

Serve the falafels with the miso garlic tahini, salad, pickled chillies and some flatbread.

CHINESE ROAST DUCK LEGS

with passion-fruit pickled cucumber & sprouted seeds

Blanching and drying the duck legs may seem like a meticulous process, but it's the best way to guarantee that crispy, mahogany lacquered finish.

Serves 2

For the duck
2 duck legs
1 litre chicken stock
150ml rice vinegar
3 tablespoons each of soy sauce
   and clear honey
1 orange, thinly sliced

For the dry rub mix
1 teaspoon each of salt, sugar, ground
   star anise, ground cinnamon crushed
   Szechuan peppercorns, finely chopped
   orange peel and fresh ginger

For the glaze
50g honey
2 teaspoons rice vinegar
1 tablespoon soy sauce

Loosen the duck skin with your fingers. Using some string, tie the legs securely to a metal coat hanger (this is my DIY version of a duck hook!). Place the stock in a large pan and bring it to the boil. Add the rice vinegar, soy sauce, honey and orange slices. Hold the coat hanger over the pan, dangling the legs in. Remove the legs from the liquid and allow to dry slightly for a few minutes (hanging over the sink is a good idea). Repeat this dunking and drying process 6–7 times.

Reserve the stock and, once cooled, chill in the fridge overnight. Mix the dry rub ingredients together, pat all over the legs and chill them overnight too.

Next day, preheat the oven to 150°C/gas mark 2. Heat all the glaze ingredients in a small pan. Place the duck legs in a roasting tin, paint the glaze over them and roast for 15 minutes in the oven. Repeat this glazing and roasting process 3 more times (roasting for an hour in total) until the duck has a thick, toffee-like coating. Raise the oven temperature to 180°C/gas mark 5. Heat the reserved stock until boiling and pour into the roasting tin. Place the legs on a rack over the roasting tin, ensuring the liquid and legs don't touch. Roast for 10–15 minutes, until crisp.

For the pickled cucumber and sprouted seeds
¼ red onion
1 tablespoon rice vinegar
100g rice noodles
½ cucumber, cut into matchsticks
2 big handfuls of bean sprouts
1 carrot, cut into matchsticks
1 tablespoon toasted sesame seeds

For the dressing
pulp from 1 passion fruit
1 teaspoon sugar
2 teaspoons each of sesame oil and
   rice vinegar
1 teaspoon grated fresh root ginger
1 garlic clove, crushed
2 teaspoons soy sauce
1 tablespoon rice bran or groundnut oil

Place the red onion in a dish with the rice vinegar and 1 tablespoon of water. Set aside for 30 minutes. Cook and drain the rice noodles. Toss the remaining ingredients together.

Combine the dressing ingredients in a small jug. Stir well and pour over the salad just before serving.

MINI CHICKEN & MUSHROOM PIES

yay!

Who doesn't adore a nice pie? Especially one with a home-made, thyme flecked pastry, fresh herbs, creamy chicken and garlicky mushrooms. If you feel cheated when something is called a pie but is all pastry lid and no bottom; this is for you.

Makes 12

For the pastry
90g butter, plus extra for greasing
200g flour, plus extra for dusting
2 heaped teaspoons dried thyme
pinch of salt

Preheat the oven to 180˚C/gas mark 4. Butter a 12-hole muffin tray and line with 12 little crumpled circles of greaseproof paper. Place the butter, flour, thyme and salt in a bowl. Rub in the butter to form breadcrumbs, bring together with a little cold water to form a dough. Wrap and chill in the fridge for 15 minutes.

On a floured surface roll out the pastry to a thickness of ¼cm. Cut into 12 circles about 10cm in diameter using a pastry cutter, small saucer or big teacup and use to line the muffin tin. Line each pastry case with a 12cm circle of baking parchment, add some baking beans and bake for 15 minutes. Remove the paper and beans and cool. Raise the oven temperature to 200˚C/gas 6.

For the filling
25g butter
2 tablespoons plain flour
300ml chicken stock
2 tablespoons olive oil
2 shallots, finely chopped
1 garlic clove, crushed
4 skinless and boneless chicken thighs,
    diced into bite-size pieces
200g closed cup or chestnut
    mushrooms, sliced
75ml white wine or dry cider
1–2 teaspoons Dijon mustard
squeeze of lemon juice
1 tablespoon chopped fresh sage leaves
1–2 tablespoons chopped fresh herbs
    e.g. rosemary, parsley,tarragon
2 tablespoons double cream
1 teaspoon each of smoked salt and freshly
    ground black pepper
375g ready rolled all-butter puff pastry
1 egg, beaten

Melt the butter gently in a medium saucepan and stir in the flour with a wooden spoon for about 5 minutes or until golden to cook out the flour and create a roux base. Gradually add the chicken stock and stir until you have a thick sauce.

In a non-stick frying pan, heat the oil and fry the shallots, garlic and diced chicken for 3 minutes. Add the mushrooms and cook until the chicken turns white and the mushrooms are cooked through. Throw in the wine or cider and cook for 3 minutes until reduced by half. Scrape the chicken and mushroom mixture into the chicken stock sauce and reduce further if you feel the sauce isn't quite thick enough. Add the Dijon mustard, lemon juice, sage and fresh herbs. Stir in the double cream and season with smoked salt and pepper.

On a floured work surface unroll the puff pastry. Cut it into 12 circles approximately 8cm in diameter. Fill the cooled pastry cases with the pie filling. Top with the circles of puff pastry, crimping well and brush with beaten egg. Bake for 20–30 minutes until golden brown.

GREEN APPLE SOM TUM

The archetypal Thai street food, Som Tum is usually a classic mouthwatering combo of sour lime, sweet palm sugar, salty umami fish sauce and hot chilli. If you're lucky enough to live near an ethnic food shop or market where you can get hold of fresh green papaya this is a fantastic, fresh way to eat it. Otherwise I've found that a couple of tart green apples make a refreshing, if not even tastier alternative. In Thailand this is always made to order, as personal preferences are so variable. So make sure you adjust the seasoning according to how salty, sour, sweet or spicy you like it.

Serves 2

2–3 garlic cloves
1½ tablespoons palm or brown sugar
1 bird's eye or green chilli, finely chopped
1½ tablespoons Thai fish sauce
juice of ½ lime

5 vine tomatoes, diced
handful of green beans or long beans, sliced
2 cooking apples, grated
2 carrots, grated
2 tablespoons unsalted peanuts, toasted

Crush the garlic with a pestle and mortar and add the sugar, chilli, fish sauce and lime juice. Pound the ingredients together. Transfer the mixture to a large bowl.

Add the tomatoes and beans and lightly pound. Stir in the grated apple and carrot and mix well.

In a dry frying pan over a medium heat, gently toast the peanuts for 5 minutes.

Sprinkle with the peanuts and serve.

SMOKED ANYA POTATO SALAD
with herrings & crème fraîche

Smoking the potatoes provides an interesting twist to this classic salad, making it a truly excellent contribution to any picnic or barbecue. My method uses the hob, but if you happen to be firing up the hot coals, just smoke the potatoes wrapped in foil over the top instead. It's not always easy to get hold of dill, so use chives or parsley instead. Try and use the most glamorous spuds you can, and make it a couple of hours in advance of eating to allow the flavours to mingle and connect.

Serves 4-6

750g Anya potatoes (or other gourmet
    potatoes e.g. Yukon Gold or Pink Fir)
1 litre vegetable or chicken stock
1 tablespoon tea leaves
1 tablespoon rice
1 tablespoon salt
2 tablespoons chopped fresh dill

275g jar pickled herrings in sweet
    onion marinade, drained
1 tablespoon chopped gherkins
200ml crème fraîche
250g Greek yogurt
1 apple
2 spring onions, finely chopped
salt and freshly ground black pepper

Pour the stock into a medium pan, bring to the boil and add the potatoes, cook for 20–25 minutes or until tender. Drain.

Scatter a large roasting dish with the tea leaves, rice and salt. Place a wire rack in the dish and arrange the potatoes on top of this. Layer a double thickness of foil over everything (including the underside of the tin) and crimp well to seal. Cover tightly with a couple more sheets and place over a medium to low hob. Turn off your smoke alarm and leave the potatoes to smoke for 15 minutes.

Unwrap and roughly dice the potatoes. Mix with the dill, herrings, gherkins, crème fraîche and yogurt.

Core and dice the apple and add to the salad along with the spring onions, salt and pepper. Adjust the seasoning and chill.

CLOTTED CREAM DOUGHNUTS

with pineapple curd

If you're going to have a doughnut, you might as well go the whole hog and lob some clotted cream into the mix – you'll be rewarded with an introduction to the lightest and fluffiest member of the fried dough family. The pineapple curd gives a good zip of sharpness to complement matters nicely. These are perfect for taking into the office when it's someone's birthday – whether or not you can bear to part with them is another matter entirely...!

Makes 14

For the doughnuts
1 tablespoon active dried yeast
55g vanilla sugar
175ml clotted cream
¼ teaspoon salt
50g butter, melted
1 large egg, beaten
225g plain flour
sunflower or rice bran oil, for deep frying

Mix all the doughnut ingredients in a bowl to form a dough, cover with clingfilm and leave for an hour.

Heat the oil to 190°C in a large saucepan or deep-fat fryer and fry the dough in batches of 4–5 tablespoonfuls at a time for 3–5 minutes or until golden and cooked through. Drain well on kitchen paper. Repeat to cook the remaining doughnuts.

For the curd
5½ tablespoons cornflour
180ml pineapple juice
6 large egg yolks
75g caster sugar
80g butter

For the curd, mix the cornflour with a little of the pineapple juice until it forms a paste. Whisk the yolks, remaining pineapple juice and sugar in a pan. Keep on a low heat and stir until thickened. Add the cornflour, stir well then add the butter and stir until melted. Chill in the fridge to firm.

Halve the doughnuts and fill them with the pineapple curd, or if you want to be really flash, carefully inject it into the centre of the doughnuts with a syringe or fine nozzle on a piping bag. Serve immediately.

You can keep any leftover pineapple curd in the fridge for a couple of weeks – it's smashing on toast or in little tarts.

FRANGIPANE NASHI PEAR TART

sweet!

The almost melon-like juiciness and perfumed flesh of the Nashi pear is such a delicate treat and one that complements a ginger nutty frangipane deliciously. The multitasking frangipane soaks up the high water content of the pears, thus protecting the pastry base. Happiness in every layer, a cinch to make and a sweet little packed lunch treat.

Serves 6-8
butter, for greasing

For the fruit
juice of ½ lemon juice
4 nashi (Asian) pears, peeled, cored and sliced into crescents

1 piece of grapefruit peel
1 star anise
1 cinnamon stick
50g sugar
2 tablespoons clear honey, plus extra for brushing

Preheat the oven to 180°C/gas mark 4. Grease and line a 24cm pie dish with greaseproof paper.

Squeeze the lemon juice over the pears and place in a small saucepan. Cover with cold water and add the grapefruit peel, star anise, cinnamon stick and sugar. Simmer gently for 15 minutes and then set aside to cool.

For the frangipane
125g butter
125 caster sugar
40g ground almonds

90g ground walnuts
5 nuggets of stem ginger in syrup, drained and finely chopped
2 eggs

Cream together the butter and sugar until smooth. Mix in the ground almonds and walnuts, stem ginger and eggs.

For the pastry
30g chopped walnuts
85g butter

170g plain flour, plus extra for dusting
50g sugar
25ml milk

Toast the walnuts in a hot, non-stick, dry frying pan until fragrant. Set aside to cool a little and then chop finely. Rub the butter into the flour, then stir in the sugar and walnuts. Gradually add enough milk to form a smooth dough. Roll out the pastry between two sheets of clingfilm to a circle 26cm in diameter and line a 24cm pie dish with the pastry. Chill for 15 minutes. Line the pastry case with greaseproof paper, add some baking beans or lentils and bake blind for 30 minutes. Remove the paper and beans and bake for a further 10 minutes. Leave to cool.

Spread the frangipane mixture over the base of the pastry case. Drain the pear slices and mix well with the honey and arrange in a fan shape over the frangipane mixture. Bake for about 40 minutes or until golden and bubbling. Brush with a little warmed honey before serving.

SUPERBERRY LOAF

with chocolate almond butter crust

A generous, fruit-encrusted loaf smeared with a thick coating of homemade chocolate almond butter makes for ruddy excellent outdoor eating. The chocolate almond butter alone is sinfully addictive and should probably come with some sort health warning, but then, you have all that fruit for balance. A guaranteed cakehole pleaser, even if the weather should (and let's face it, probably will) let you down.

Serves 6-8

For the chocolate almond butter
200g almonds
1 heaped teaspoon sea salt
100g milk chocolate, roughly broken

Preheat the oven to 180°C/gas mark 4. Line a 900g loaf tin with crumpled baking parchment.

Toast the almonds in a hot, non-stick, dry frying pan until they are fragrant and golden. Transfer them to a food processor and add the salt. Process for about 10 minutes, they'll look a bit 'floury' at first, but keep scraping down the sides and eventually you'll be left with a nutty butter. Set aside.

For the cake
250g self-raising flour
150g caster sugar
1 teaspoon baking powder
2 medium eggs, lightly beaten
1 teaspoon vanilla extract
150g natural yogurt
130g butter, melted
zest of 2 limes
60g strawberries, roughly chopped
60g blueberries
60g raspberries
60g blackberries
1 tablespoon demerara sugar, to sprinkle
75g icing sugar

Mix the flour, caster sugar and baking powder together in a bowl. In a separate bowl, mix the eggs, vanilla extract, yogurt, melted butter and lime zest together thoroughly. Fold into the flour mixture and stir in the berries. Pour the lot into the loaf tin and sprinkle with the demerara sugar. Cook for 45–50 minutes, until well risen and golden. Leave in the tin for 15 minutes and then cool on a wire rack.

Place the chocolate pieces in a heatproof bowl over a pan of gently simmering water and stir until melted. Stir the chocolate into the almond butter, taste and add more salt if necessary. Spread the butter over the top and sides of the cooled loaf and leave until it sets hard.

Slice and scoff with gluttonous abandon.

This will keep in an airtight container for about 4 days.

PARTY FUEL

FOR THE UNINSPIRED!

It can be such a tricky one, knowing what to serve when you're planning a bit of a get together. On the one hand, you don't want to offer lame old bowls of crisps around, and even though there's something deliciously retro about a cheese and pineapple hedgehog, there are times when you want to come up with that extra special something on a stick.

Also, on a more practical level, you're after the sort of scran that will mop up any excess booze and avoid people getting too wasted, too quickly. Having said all of that, the ultimate goal is to show your mates a good time. Salted Honey Popcorn and Tandoori Fried Chicken are all pretty much guaranteed ice breakers and will help encourage everyone to get all euphoric in the mouth – finger foods that you can eat with a drink in one hand.

You want good time grub that people just can't get enough of and snacks that kick off the night with a tango on the tastebuds. You know, that sort of food.

GOUDA & CUMIN GOUGÈRES

tasty!

All hail the mighty French cheesy puff. I challenge anyone with correctly functioning olfactory glands to resist these ethereal explosions of glory. You don't have to use Gouda, any strong nutty cheese works wonders. When you add the eggs do it off the heat so they don't scramble and make sure the gougères have a good, golden hue running up the sides before you pluck them from the oven, to ensure they don't deflate. Gougères can also be baked straight from the freezer (allow a few extra minutes in the oven) so you can make a tray full well in advance, if you're an organised type. To make stuffed savoury profiteroles, mix cream cheese, chives and finely diced smoked fish or meat and pipe artfully into the middle of each cooled gougère (or just halve and sandwich together).

Makes 24

45g butter, plus extra for greasing
1 teaspoon cumin seeds, roughly crushed
½ teaspoon salt
freshly ground black pepper

pinch of cayenne pepper
70g plain flour
2 eggs, beaten
100g mature Gouda cheese, grated

Preheat the oven to 220°C/gas mark 7. Line 2 baking sheets with baking paper and grease well.

Place the butter, cumin, salt, pepper and cayenne pepper in a medium pan with 125ml water and heat until the butter melts. Add the flour and mix vigorously over the heat until the mixture forms a smooth dough. Make sure you really beat that mixture – go on, show it who's boss!

Take off the heat, cool for a couple of minutes and gradually add the beaten eggs, mixing well until smooth. Add the cheese and mix until completely combined.

Either pipe from a piping bag using a wide plain nozzle, or blob teaspoonfuls of the mixture onto the prepared baking sheets. Bake for 10 minutes and then reduce the oven temperature to 190°C/gas mark 5 and bake for a further 15-20 minutes until golden and puffy. Serve hot or cold with drinks.

SESAME GARLIC EDAMAME

Those little pods of pre-boiled and salted edamame must be one of most overpriced things you can purchase from a chiller counter. Mine take the usual salted pods a step further and are the easiest thing ever to chuck together. You can buy frozen edamame pods online or from Oriental supermarkets. They're a great little freezer standby as you can cook them in 5 minutes straight from frozen, perfect for those unexpected impromptu visits when the fridge is bare. These are addictively good and proof that delicious party food doesn't have to be unhealthy or cost the earth.

Serves 4-6

450g frozen edamame pods
1 tablespoon sesame oil
2–3 garlic cloves, crushed
1 tablespoon sesame seeds

1 dessertspoon soy sauce
1 dessertspoon rice vinegar
1 teaspoon sugar
1 teaspoon salt
dried chilli flakes, to taste

Cook the edamame according to the pack instructions (usually chuck in to a large pan of salted boiling water, cook for 5 minutes then drain).

Meanwhile, heat the sesame oil in a small pan and gently fry the garlic until golden. Add the sesame seeds and when everything is fragrant and toasted, remove from the heat and stir in the soy sauce, rice vinegar, sugar, salt and chilli flakes.

Pour over the drained edamame, stirring well to ensure every pod is well coated. Serve warm with plenty of chilled beer.

STUFFED QUAIL'S EGGS

with homemade gentleman's relish

For me, there are few things more conducive to a weak-kneed moment than those marinated anchovies you get on deli counters. If you're a fan of the tangy little fishies then this is definitely the canapé for you. Very loosely based on the original patum peperium, my recipe carries a much sharper, more vinegary punch, undercut with the mellow hum of mace. So basically nothing like the bland, dun-coloured pap you get in those little pots, and an unremitting thrill on hot, buttered toast.

Makes 24

12 quail's eggs
150g butter
100g marinated anchovies
1 tablespoon capers in brine, chopped
few drops of chilli sauce

½ teaspoon cayenne pepper
½ teaspoon mace
freshly ground black pepper
freshly grated nutmeg, to taste
lemon juice, to taste
1 tablespoon finely chopped fresh parsley

Heat a pan of water and as soon as it has started to boil, add the quail's eggs and cook for 2½ minutes. Drain and run the eggs under cold water. Peel and halve the eggs and remove the yolks.

Melt the butter in a small pan and add the anchovies, capers, chilli sauce, cayenne and mace. Stir well and season to taste with black pepper, nutmeg and lemon juice. Using a teaspoon carefully fill the yolk cavities with the anchovy mixture. Sprinkle with chopped parsley and leave to set in the fridge.

Spoon any excess relish in a ramekin, chill to set and serve with hot, buttered, crustless white toast.

 # TFC

tandoori fried chicken

Crunchy, spicy and finger licking fun – it's always a cracking idea to set a tone of unbridled informality with something a bit messy, something glistening, something that you need to gnaw with your hands and get down your top. Serve with very cold drinks and plenty of napkins.

Serves 3-4

For the marinade
1 teaspoon cumin seeds
1 teaspoon coriander seeds
284ml buttermilk or natural yogurt
1 teaspoon curry powder
1 teaspoon chilli powder or ½ green chilli,
    finely chopped
1 teaspoon freshly ground black pepper

2-3 tablespoons finely chopped fresh
    coriander
½ medium onion, grated
8 garlic cloves, crushed
2.5cm piece fresh root ginger, grated
4 tablespoons tomato purée
1 tablespoon sugar
½ teaspoon cayenne pepper
1 teaspoon sea salt

Toast the cumin and coriander seeds in a non-stick frying pan until fragrant. Grind the toasted seeds to a powder using a pestle and mortar. Combine the spice powder with the remaining marinade ingredients in a large bowl.

For the chicken
4 chicken thighs, skin on
4 chicken drumsticks, skin on
groundnut oil and beef dripping (optional),
    for frying

150g rice flour
1 teaspoon cayenne pepper
1 teaspoon smoked paprika
1 teaspoon sea salt
2 teaspoons freshly ground black pepper

Make several slashes in the chicken flesh and coat with the marinade. Cover and refrigerate overnight.

Preheat the oven to 200°C/gas mark 6. Pat the chicken dry to remove any excess liquid. In a bowl or paper bag combine the flour, cayenne pepper, smoked paprika, salt and pepper. Place the beaten egg in a shallow dish.

Place each piece of chicken, one at a time, in the seasoned flour and coat well, then dip the chicken into the egg. Place the chicken back into the flour to coat for a second time. Repeat this for all the chicken pieces.

Heat 2.5cm of oil with the beef dripping (if using) in a large heavy-bottomed pan over a medium-high heat until it reaches 190°C or a cube of bread browns almost instantly. Tap off the excess flour and fry a couple of pieces at a time for approximately 4–5 minutes until golden brown all over. Transfer the chicken pieces to a baking tray. Cover loosely with foil. Repeat with the remaining chicken.

Transfer to the oven and bake for 25–30 minutes until the juices run clear.

ROAST DUCK BANH MI

quack!

Utterly gorgeous, this is one of those sarnies that has you craving another immediately after and still reminiscing about it days later. Banh Mi are traditionally made with rice flour baguettes, which are a bit of a palaver to source, so just use a fresh baguette that you've heated in the oven for that freshness factor. I've used a confit method with the duck legs, but with Chinese flavours for a real melt in the mouth extravaganza (if you keep the fat for the next batch, it just improves each time). Seriously stunning.

Serves 2

For the spice paste and duck
1 teaspoon ground cinnamon
4 cloves
1 teaspoon fennel seeds
2–3 star anise
1 teaspoon Szechuan peppercorns
salt

1 tablespoon honey
1 tablespoon soy sauce
1 tablespoon Thai fish sauce
4 garlic cloves, crushed
2.5cm piece fresh root ginger, grated
2 duck legs
olive oil or melted duck fat

Grind the cinnamon, cloves, fennel seed, star anise, Szechuan peppercorns and salt in a spice mill or pestle and mortar until you have a fine powder. Mix this powder with the honey, soy sauce, fish sauce, garlic and ginger to a fragrant paste. Rub the paste all over the duck legs then place in a non-metallic container, cover and chill in the fridge, at least overnight and up to two days ahead of cooking.

Confit the duck legs by placing them skin-side down in a pan (they should fit snugly in a single layer) and pouring over the olive oil or melted duck fat to immerse completely. Cook over the lowest heat for 2 hours, after which the meat will be unbelievably tender.

Preheat the oven to 200°C/gas mark 6. Remove the duck legs from the oil or fat (reserve the fat for next time) and transfer to a roasting tin. Roast the duck for 40 minutes or until very crisp. Shred the duck and cool to room temperature.

For the pickles
4 tablespoons rice vinegar
2 teaspoons salt

2 teaspoons sugar
2 carrots, cut into matchsticks
3 small beetroot, cut into matchsticks

Mix the rice vinegar, salt and sugar together until the sugar dissolves and pour over the carrot and beetroot matchsticks, mixing well. Leave for 1 hour.

For the chilli miso mayo
1 tablespoon chilli sauce
1 tablespoon Thai fish sauce
1 tablespoon red miso paste

2 spring onions, finely chopped
2 tablespoons finely chopped fresh
   coriander
2 tablespoons mayonnaise

Combine all the ingredients in a small bowl and mix well.

To serve
2 baguettines or a standard baguette

jalapeños, finely sliced, to taste

To serve, warm the bread in the oven, split in half lengthways and spread with some chilli miso mayonnaise, shredded duck, pickled vegetables and sliced jalapeños. Serve with a blob of the mayonnaise on the side to dunk, plus the remaining pickles.

STUFFED-CRUST SPICY LAMB PIDE

mmm!

This brings together the finest aspects of pizza nirvana – namely spicy lamb Anatolian pizza taken one step beyond with a cheese and herb stuffed border. A good veggie alternative is caramelised onions, grilled feta and sautéed potato slices, or smoked aubergine and red peppers with spinach, cheese and parsley. Whatever you go for, that pleasing yawn of stretchy fromage as you cut into the crust is unbeatable.

Makes 2 large pides

For the dough
150ml milk
1 teaspoon active dried yeast
1 egg, beaten

1 teaspoon sugar
1 teaspoon salt
3 tablespoons olive oil
350g strong plain flour

Preheat the oven to 240°C/gas mark 9. Line 2 baking trays with baking paper.

Heat the milk gently for a few minutes so that it's just warm but not so hot that you kill the yeast. Pour the milk into a medium bowl and stir in the yeast to dissolve. Add the beaten egg, sugar, salt and oil. Mix everything well and stir in the flour. Knead for about 5 minutes until you have a pliant, supple dough. Place the dough in an oiled bowl and cover with clingfilm or a plastic bag and leave somewhere warm for at least 30 minutes until doubled in size.

Divide the dough into two balls. Roll each ball out into a thin oval approximately 30 x 20cm. Place the ovals onto the baking trays.

For the topping
40g butter
1 tablespoon olive oil
1 medium onion, chopped
3 garlic cloves, finely chopped
400g minced lamb
1 teaspoon ground cumin
½ teaspoon paprika
2 teaspoons salt
1–2 teaspoons harissa paste
1 fresh green chilli, finely chopped
2 teaspoons dried chilli flakes
1-2 tablespoons lemon juice

freshly ground black pepper
2 tablespoons finely chopped fresh parsley
2 tablespoons finely chopped fresh mint
     leaves or 2 teaspoons dried mint
4–5 pickled chillies, chopped
½ red onion, diced
1 medium tomato, diced
2–3 roasted red peppers from a jar, diced
250g mozzarella cheese, grated
1 tablespoon finely chopped fresh parsley or
     chives
beaten egg, milk or olive oil, to glaze

Melt 30g of the butter in a large non-stick frying pan, add the oil and onion and two-thirds of the chopped garlic. Cook for 5 minutes or until softened, then add the lamb, cumin, paprika, salt, harissa, fresh green chilli and chilli flakes and continue to cook for 8-10 minutes or until the lamb is well browned. Remove from the heat and leave to cool slightly.

Add the lemon juice, black pepper, parsley, mint, pickled chillies, red onion, tomato and red peppers to the pan and stir well.

Mash the remaining 10g of butter with the remaining chopped garlic and some salt. Melt the garlic butter in a small pan or in the microwave. Brush the edges of each dough oval with the melted garlic butter and line with a rim of grated mozzarella and some parsley or chives. Fold this over itself to form a stuffed crust and fill the inside of each oval with half the lamb mixture. Top with the remaining mozzarella and brush the dough with beaten egg, milk or olive oil to glaze.

Bake for 15–20 minutes, or until the dough is golden and the cheese bubbling. Serve immediately.

CHILLI, LIME & FETA STUFFED SQUID

with Thai watermelon salad

Squid is now far more readily available than even just a couple of years ago, and it's a great sustainable alternative to so many of the other over-fished options available to us. It's also nice and cheap. This makes for excellent party fare because you can flash grill it to the tenderest effect, for ultra tropical fun times. I love the way Thais chuck all manner of fruit in their salads. Here sweet, juicy watermelon goes brilliantly with the smoky feta-stuffed cephalopod, while the plucky dressing evocatively conjures up the Phuketian spirit.

Serves 6

For the pickles
1 teaspoon sugar
1 teaspoon salt
90ml rice vinegar
½ red onion, diced
2 carrots, cut into batons
½ cucumber, cut into batons

Dissolve the sugar and salt in the rice vinegar. Add the red onion, carrot and cucumber and set aside for 30 minutes.

For the salad
juice of ½ a lime
1 tablespoon Thai fish sauce
½ teaspoon grated garlic
1 teaspoon grated fresh root ginger
½ tablespoon soy sauce
½ teaspoon sugar
1 tablespoon rice vinegar
1 fresh coconut, flesh finely chopped (optional)
½ fresh watermelon, cut into chunks
2 tablespoons roughly chopped fresh coriander
25g toasted peanuts (optional)

To make the dressing, combine the lime juice, fish sauce, garlic, ginger, soy sauce, sugar and rice vinegar. Set aside.

In a large bowl combine the coconut (if using), watermelon, coriander and peanuts (if using) with the pickled red onion, carrot and cucumber. Set aside.

For the squid
1 heaped teaspoon cumin seeds
zest of 1 lime
juice of ½ a lime
1 tablespoon olive oil
1 green chilli, finely chopped
½ red onion, finely sliced
2 garlic cloves, crushed
6 x 250g squid tubes, cleaned
200g feta cheese

Toast the cumin seeds in a non-stick frying pan until fragrant. Grind the toasted seeds to a powder using a pestle and mortar. Mix the powder with the lime zest, lime juice, olive oil, green chilli, red onion and garlic. Place the squid in a non-metallic container and pour over the marinade. Chill in the fridge for a minimum of 3 hours.

Place the red onions from the marinade into a bowl and mash with the feta. Stuff two-thirds of each squid with this mixture and secure with cocktail sticks (take care not to overstuff as the squid will shrink slightly when cooked).

Heat a griddle pan over a medium heat. Shake any excess marinade from the squid and cook for 2-3 minutes on each side until the feta melts and the squid is branded with ebony lines of char.

Pour the dressing over the salad, plonk the squid on top and serve immediately.

HAZELNUT CHOC ICES

Oooh the indulgence. If you can't treat yourself at a party, then when can you? If you harbour a secret nut addiction and would like to incorporate this in a frozen choc ice, then look no further. Yes, they're a bit of a faff to make and, okay, so they look more like frozen cupcakes than actual rectangular choc ices, but oh my goodness they're more than worth it. Far too good to save for the sunshiney months.

Makes 12

250ml whole milk
4 teaspoons custard powder
250ml double cream
½ teaspoon vanilla extract
30g dark chocolate, roughly broken
100ml hazelnut cream liqueur

60g crunchy peanut butter
1 teaspoons salt
oil, for greasing
50g hazelnuts
300g milk chocolate, roughly broken
6 Ferrero Rochers

Stick a 12-hole muffin tray in the freezer. Mix a little of the milk with the custard powder to form a paste. In a saucepan, heat the remaining milk with the cream and the vanilla extract. Once it comes to the boil reduce the heat, add the chocolate and custard paste and cook gently for about 5 minutes, until the chocolate has melted.

Take off the heat, stir in the cream liqueur, peanut butter and salt and churn in an ice cream maker until set. Alternatively put the mixture into a plastic container and freeze until set, stirring every 30 minutes to prevent crystals from forming.

Line the chilled muffin tray with lightly oiled muffin cases and fill with the ice cream. Freeze for a couple of hours, or until you have solid 'cakes'.

Toast the hazelnuts in a non-stick frying pan. Roughly crush using a pestle and mortar.

Place the milk chocolate into a heatproof bowl over a pan of gently simmering water and stir until melted. Allow to cool a little. Crush the Ferrero Rochers with a pestle and mortar and mix them into the melted chocolate.

Prepare a further 12 muffin cases by lightly oiling each one and sprinkling with half of the crushed hazelnuts.

Working quickly, insert a lolly stick into each choc ice, remove the frozen choc ices from the muffin tray and replace each one with a nut-lined empty cases. Peel the greased cases from each choc ice and spoon the melted chocolate over the bottom of each one until well coated. Put the choc ices straight into the nut-lined muffin cases so that each one is semi-covered in nuts and chocolate. Sprinkle the top of each choc ice with the remaining crushed hazelnuts and smother quickly in the remaining melted chocolate. Freeze again until needed.

CARDAMOM & BLACKBERRY CHOCOLATE MOUSSE CAKE

This can be made a day or so in advance, and because it's so rich you only need to serve the weeniest portions. Très sophisticated, mousse-like and appallingly chocolatey, this is just the thing for those times when you want to be decadent and celebratory.

Serves 16

For the cake
175g butter, plus extra for greasing
300g milk chocolate, roughly broken
1 teaspoon sea salt
180g caster sugar
3 whole cardamom pods
2 large eggs
2 tablespoons ground almonds
2 tablespoons blackberry jam

Preheat the oven to 180°C/gas mark 4. Grease and line a 20cm springfrom cake tin with baking paper.

Place the butter, chocolate, salt, sugar and cardamom pods in a large heatproof bowl over a pan of gently simmering water and stir until melted.

Whisk the eggs and fold into the mixture, along with the ground almonds. Fold until nice and thick, pour into the prepared tin and bake for 30–40 minutes. Leave in the tin to cool thoroughly. Spread the cooled cake with the jam.

For the mousse
9 cardamom pods
250g dark chocolate, roughly broken
175g butter
100g icing sugar, sifted
4 large eggs, separated
150ml double cream, whipped until stiff,
    plus extra to serve
150g blackberries, plus extra to serve

Remove the seeds from the cardamom pods and grind to a powder in a pestle and mortar. Place the chocolate and butter in a large heatproof bowl over a pan of gently simmering water and stir until melted. Add half the icing sugar, the egg yolks and the cardamom powder. Stir and set aside.

Whisk the egg whites to form stiff peaks, fold in the remaining icing sugar and carefully fold into the chocolate mixture using a metal spoon. Fold in the double cream and pour the mixture over the cake base. Decorate with the fresh blackberries. Refrigerate for at least 5–6 hours or until completely set.

Serve chilled with whipped cream and extra blackberries on the side.

TOFFEE & APPLE CRUMBLE ICE CREAM

A real showstopper, this killer combo of salted toffee sauce, tart apple ice cream and hot crunchy crumble topping is a glorious mash-up of everyone's favourite sweet things.

Serves 8

For the ice cream
300ml whole milk
300ml double cream
5 large egg yolks
120g golden caster sugar
pinch freshly grated nutmeg
½ teaspoon ground cinnamon
1 teaspoon vanilla paste

Bring the milk and cream just to the boil in a small non-stick pan. Whisk the egg yolks and sugar in a bowl, and gradually mix into the milk and cream. Cook over a very low heat, stirring constantly, until the mixture starts to thicken. (Be careful not to let the mixture boil or it will split.) Remove from the heat and stir in the nutmeg, cinnamon and vanilla. Leave to cool and chill overnight. The next day, pour the chilled vanilla custard into an ice cream maker and churn until almost frozen.

For the toffee sauce
100g butter
250g demerara sugar
200ml single cream
2 teaspoons vanilla extract
1 heaped teaspoon sea salt

Slowly melt the butter and sugar in a heavy-based pan until golden and caramelised. Pour in the cream (stand back as it will bubble up!) and stir in the vanilla and salt. Remove from the heat, leave to cool and chill overnight.

For the apple
2 cooking apples, peeled, cored and cubed
juice of ½ lemon
30g butter

Sprinkle the apples with the lemon juice. Melt the butter in a frying pan. Add the apple cubes and cook until just soft and tender, but still a little tart. Leave to cool and chill overnight.

For the crumble
50g pecans
50g almonds
90g butter
175g self raising flour
90g golden caster sugar

Preheat the oven to 180°C/gas mark 4. Grind the nuts in a food processor. Rub the butter into the flour until it forms crumbs. Rub in the sugar until it starts to form clumps. Stir in the ground nuts and then tip the lot onto a baking sheet. Bake for 15-20 minutes or until golden and biscuit-like. Leave to cool.

Gently fold the apple pieces into the ice cream followed by half the crumble. Pour half of the the salted toffee sauce over the ice cream and gently fold to create a ripple effect. Heat the remaining toffee sauce in a pan and serve the ice cream topped with the remaining crumble mixture and the hot toffee sauce.

SALTED HONEY POPCORN

pop! pop! pop!

Are you one of those people that likes to go for a half and half salty sweet mix of popcorn? If so, you'll go doolally for this. Use whatever honey you have to hand – it's all about that salty sweet contrast. Having ruined many a popcorn pan in my time, I've finally come up with the definitive kernel popping method. This is one of the best ways of avoiding those blackened, unpopped molar-cracking kernels of shame that can so often be the blight of a good batch.

Serves 4

1 tablespoon coconut or avocado oil or any other robust, high heat-withstanding oil

250g popcorn kernels (enough to coat the base of a large pan in a single layer)
50g butter
50g honey
1–2 teaspoons salt

Heat the oil in a large lidded saucepan over a medium-low heat and drop in 3 kernels of corn. As soon as all 3 pop (this can take a few minutes) remove from the heat and pour in the remaining kernels. Cover tightly with the lid.

Shake the kernels vigorously for 30 seconds and then return to the heat and leave for the remaining corn to get busily clattering and exploding. Remove from the heat as soon as this slows down.

In a small pan, melt the butter and stir in the honey and salt. Pour over the popcorn and mix well. Devour immediately.

THERE, THERE, THERE

Ufff. You promised yourself this would never happen again, but here you are. The blistering throb behind blood-shot eyes. The porridge-like head fug of flu. Or just the general bleakness that sets in after completely self-saturating with endless fat, animal matter, salt and other Very Bad Things.

There's nothing more debilitating than feeling under the weather, and sometimes you need a lot more than the saline plink, plink fizz of recuperation. Sometimes what you really need is a little TLC for the tastebuds, body and soul. A spot of retox detox if you like, in the form of hot and sour chillified greenery, followed perhaps with some coconut churros to balance out the system with a much needed saccharine surge reboot. Because it doesn't have to be all sanctimonious rabbit food — the road to recovery should absolutely be a joyfully tasty one. As someone famous once said, the mediator between the brain and muscle must be the heart. There's a lot to be said for negotiating that harmonious path between an oral endorphin rush and the rest of the body bearing solemn witness to your fitness.

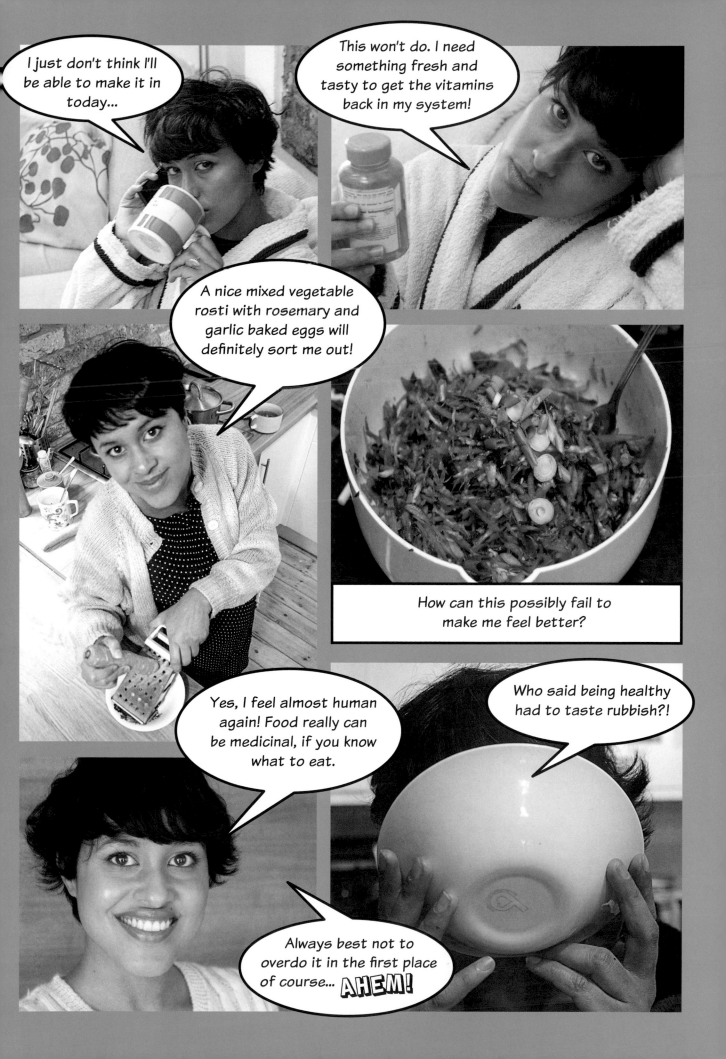

NECTARINE & TOMATO GAZPACHO

cool!

If the very mention of the word España evokes plastic tables in the sun, people-watching and losing yourself in a chilled, garlicky bowl of the mouth-popping wonder that is gazpacho then this is the recovery dish for you. Nectarines provide a refreshing twist, the sweetness really ekes out the best in the tomatoes. If you're lucky enough to get your mitts on some tarragon, then rip it in with abandon. Otherwise, parsley is very much your friend. The secret to this is in the lengthy chilling so make it as far in advance as you can possibly bear to wait, and serve very, very cold. A taste sensation that's too good to save for when you're feeling peaky. Sup enough of this and you're pretty much guaranteed to never succumb to that treacherous state in the first place.

Serves 4

4-5 medium very fresh, ripe tomatoes
3 nectarines or 4 doughnut
    peaches, stoned
3 tablespoons extra virgin olive oil
1½ tablespoons chopped fresh
    tarragon, dill or parsley
2 teaspoons salt
freshly ground black pepper

½ tablespoon balsamic vinegar
1½ tablespoons sherry vinegar or red
    wine vinegar
½ red pepper, deseeded
½ yellow pepper, deseeded
½ green pepper, deseeded
¼ red onion
2 garlic cloves, crushed

Place all the ingredients in a food processor or blender and blitz, leaving some texture.

Check and adjust seasoning. Chill and serve with ice cubes.

HOT & SOUR CABBAGE & TOFU SOUP

Greens. We all know we're meant to eat more of them, but it's so hard when there are so many other delicious, less healthy things to consume of every other hue (it's usually the browns of meat, cola and chocolate that mark my downfall). I'm forever trying to think up ways to make them more appetising. Complex, spicy, salty, sour and replete with goodness, there's a different layer in every mouthful. This is one of those proper electric jump-start jolts to the system that basically high kicks your tastebuds into meek submission.

Serves 2

1 tablespoon sesame oil
6–7cm fresh root ginger, finely chopped
2 garlic cloves, finely chopped
2 spring onions, white and green parts separated, finely chopped
1 tablespoon chilli bean paste
500ml chicken stock
1 piece dried black fungus (optional)
60g shiitake mushrooms, chopped
350g soft tofu

100g cabbage, finely shredded
1 tablespoon pickled vegetables (from the chilled counter of Oriental supermarkets), optional
150g can bamboo shoots, drained
2 tablespoons rice vinegar
1 teaspoon sugar
1 tablespoon soy sauce

Heat the sesame oil in a large pan and fry the ginger, garlic and white part of the spring onions for 2–3 minutes. Add the chilli bean paste and fry for 2–3 minutes or until everything is fragrant.

Add the stock, dried fungus, shiitake mushrooms, tofu, cabbage, pickled vegetables if using and bamboo shoots. Stir in the rice vinegar and sugar and add the soy sauce to taste. Remove the dried fungus.

Serve the soup piping hot, with the green part of the spring onion sprinkled over the top.

LAO COCONUT FISH SOUP

Hot, garlicky, coconut rich, yet electric with tiny chilli explosions, this is as reviving as it gets. This khao poon recipe was passed on to me from my friend Manola's mum. Manola is Laotian and was born in Minnesota, and we taught English together in Japan. She'd simmer up a big pot of this after a big night out on the Tokyo tiles, and I remember thinking how I'd never tasted anything quite so guaranteed to recharge the old batteries.

The food of Laos is subtly different to that of Vietnam or Thailand. This is mainly because the Chinese influence hit Laos later than the other two countries, and as the country is basically landlocked, the Lao's utilised ingredients that were readily available to them, namely fresh river fish and coconuts. I tend to use defrosted frozen white fish fillets and coconut milk to replicate these.

Serves 2-4

3 teaspoons salt
2 tablespoons Thai fish sauce
6cm piece fresh galangal root or
    fresh root ginger, sliced thinly
1 lemongrass stalk
300g white fish fillets, eg coley
5-6 garlic cloves
2-3 green chillies
400ml can coconut milk
1 chicken stock cube

1 tablespoon sugar
2 x 50g sticks rice noodles or rice
    vermicelli noodles
¼ cabbage, shredded
3 carrots, julienned
100g beansprouts
1 small bunch fresh coriander, finely chopped
1 small bunch fresh mint leaves, finely
    chopped
lime wedges, fish sauce and red chopped
    chillies, to serve

Place the salt, fish sauce, galangal or ginger and lemongrass in a saucepan with 2 litres of water and bring to the boil. Add the fish and simmer for 15 minutes. Remove the fish and set aside.

Mash the garlic and chillies to a chunky paste using a pestle and mortar and mix well with the fish.

Pour the coconut milk into the saucepan, crumble in the chicken stock cube and the chilli-garlic fish. Simmer the soup for around 30 minutes. Discard the lemongrass and add the sugar.

Prepare the noodles according to the pack instructions and divide between two deep soup bowls.

Top the noodles with the cabbage, carrots and beansprouts and ladle the soup broth over. Garnish with the coriander and mint. Serve with the lime wedges, fish sauce and extra chillies to season according to personal taste.

ROASTED PUMPKIN & THREE LENTIL DHAL

Before you think, 'how long?!' about this list of ingredients, have another gander. It's really just spices, root veg, lentils, stock and canned tomatoes You'll be so absorbed in how easy it is on the tongue you'll forget how unbelievably good for you it is. Make more than you need and freeze the rest. Defrost before heading out for a big one and the next day you'll be thanking your lucky stars you did.

Serves 8-10

360g pumpkin, hacked into wedges
olive oil, for drizzling
1½ teaspoons salt
½ teaspoon turmeric
100g yellow split lentils
100g mung beans
2 onions, roughly chopped
1 bay leaf, crumbled
1 litre vegetable or chicken stock
100g red lentils
50g fresh root ginger, rougly chopped
6 garlic cloves
2-3 green chillies, roughly chopped
½ tablespoon butter or ghee
1 teaspoon mustard seeds

10-15 curry leaves
1 teaspoon cumin seeds
1 teaspoon curry powder
1 teaspoon chilli powder
½ teaspoon freshly grated nutmeg or
    1 teaspoon mace
pinch of asafoetida (optional)
400g can chopped tomatoes
pinch of sugar
2 tablespoons chopped fresh
    coriander leaves
1 green chilli, roughly chopped
lemon juice, to taste
tamarind sauce, to taste
cucumber raita and roti, to serve

Preheat the oven to 160°C/gas mark 3. Place the pumpkin wedges in a roasting tin and drizzle over some oil, sprinkle with ½ teaspoon salt and the turmeric and toss well. Roast for 1 hour or until soft and slightly caramelised in places.

Place the yellow split lentils and the mung beans in a large saucepan, add one of the roughly chopped onions, the bay leaf, a drizzle of oil, the stock and enough water to cover and bring to a boil. Reduce the heat and simmer for 1 hour. Add the red lentils and some more water and continue simmering for about 20 minutes or until all the lentils are tender. Lightly mash the pulses and add the roasted pumpkin to the pan. Blend with a hand-held electric blender and set aside.

Blitz the ginger, garlic, green chillies and the other onion to a purée in a food processor.

In a large pan, melt the ghee or butter and add a little olive oil to stop it from burning. Once it's hot, lob in the mustard seeds and once they start to protest, add the curry leaves. Chuck in the cumin seeds, curry powder, chilli powder, nutmeg or mace and asafoetida if using.

Add the blitzed onion, ginger, garlic, chilli, canned tomatoes and pumpkiny pulses to the pan. Stir well. Add 1 heaped teaspoon salt, the sugar, coriander and chilli plus lemon juice and tamarind sauce to taste. Reheat gently over a low heat until piping hot and serve with some cucumber raita and roti.

GASTROGEEK

MUSHROOM PÂTÉ

I always thought of mushroom pâté as a poor, cardboardy substitute to the proper meat versions, until I came up with this. It's addictive. If you have a stash of the wild mushroom and garlic salt from page 74, now's the time to get it out. The more exotic mushroom varieties are meant to be incredibly good for you, full of cancer busting anti-inflammatory properties, according to those canny mycologists, but this is fine with any variety of brown fungi.

Serves 4

60g butter
200g brown mushrooms, sliced
1 onion, chopped
freshly ground black pepper
juice of ½ lemon
1 teaspoon soy sauce
½ teaspoon cayenne pepper
½ teaspoon dried thyme

1 teaspoon dried sage
freshly grated nutmeg, to season
1 fat garlic clove, crushed
1 tablespoon finely chopped fresh parsley
1 teaspoon salt
1 teaspoon garlic powder or wild
   mushroom salt (see page 74)
100g cream cheese
fresh parsley sprigs, to garnish

In a medium pan, melt the butter and fry the mushrooms and onions until the onions have sweated down and the mushrooms are cooked through and have released some of their juice. Remove from the heat, season well with black pepper and stir in all the remaining ingredients bar the cream cheese. Allow to completely cool.

Transfer the vegetable mixture to a blender or food processor and add the cream cheese. Pulse to a pâté consistency.

Spoon into ramekins and serve with plenty of warm ripped up baguette and an ironic sprig of parsley or two.

HAINANESE CHICKEN RICE

Enjoyed in a variety of ways across the Far East, chicken rice is pretty much the equivalent of Asian penicillin. This simple, yet blindingly tasty combination of broth, chicken and rice means there's not really anywhere for a flaccid bird to hide, so buy the best you can afford.

Serves 4-6

For the chicken
6 chicken thighs, fat trimmed and reserved
1 tablespoon salt, plus extra for seasoning
1 tablespoon Shaoxing rice wine
4 fat garlic cloves, crushed
7cm piece fresh root ginger, finely chopped
6 spring onions, finely chopped
1 chicken stock cube
1 tablespoon soy sauce
½ tablespoon sesame oil

For the rice
300g brown basmati, jasmine or other
   long grain rice
3 teaspoons sesame oil
1 tablespoon reserved chicken fat or butter
2 shallots or 1 medium onion, finely chopped

1 tablespoon finely chopped fresh root ginger
1 tablespoon finely chopped garlic

For the chilli sauce
1 tablespoon lime juice
2 teaspoons sugar
3 tablespoons siracha chilli sauce (a tangy,
   sweet, spicy Thai chilli sauce. Alternatively,
   use Sambal olek, a thick Indonesian
   chilli sauce)
1 tablespoon chilli bean paste
2 fat garlic cloves, blitzed to a paste
3cm piece fresh root ginger, blitzed to
   a paste
1 tablespoon soy sauce
2 tablespoons coriander
1 tablespoon rice vinegar
sliced spring onions and cucumber slices,
   to serve

Soak the rice in cold water for 20 minutes. Massage the chicken all over with the salt, as if you're exfoliating it. Rinse and pat it dry – this will get rid of any impurities and ensure a good skin, which is crucial in this dish. Combine the rice wine, garlic, ginger and spring onions in a small bowl and stir well. Season the chicken generously with more salt and rub all over with the rice wine mixture.

Place the chicken in a large pan, add enough water to cover, crumble in the stock cube, semi-cover with a lid and simmer on a very gentle heat for about 50 minutes. Skim off any scum. Very carefully remove the chicken and set aside to cool.

Drain the rice. Heat the sesame oil and chicken fat or butter and fry the shallots, ginger and garlic. Stir in the rice, coating well. Add 500ml of the broth, reduce the heat and leave to cook.

Whizz up all the chilli sauce ingredients plus 2 tablespoons of the chicken broth in a blender.

Rub the chicken with a little salt, soy sauce and sesame oil, slice up. Heat up the chicken broth and add some sliced spring onions. Arrange the sliced cucumber on a plate, place pieces of the chicken on top and serve with the rice, chilli sauce and bowls of the broth.

ROASTED AUBERGINE MACARONI CHEESE

yay!

The pasta police claim that macaroni cheese should be as simple and unadulterated as possible, that there's no room for strong flavours in this dish. I couldn't disagree more. It's a proven fact that as we get older our taste buds basically die, so if you've properly nuked your senses you need something that's really going to wake them up. Adding smoked aubergine to the sauce really infuses this with a porcine top note, minus any actual pig. Easy to wang together when you're feeling fragile, this is a big, fat triple tog duvet of comfort to recover under until everything feels better again.

Serves 4

1 aubergine
300g macaroni
35g butter
25g plain flour
300ml whole milk
1 teaspoon Dijon mustard
freshly grated nutmeg, to season

½ teaspoon smoked paprika
1–2 teaspoons salt
freshly ground black pepper
90g smoked Cheddar cheese, grated
   plus extra for sprinkling
100ml double cream
1 garlic clove, crushed

Preheat the oven to 180°C/gas mark 4.

Flame roast the whole aubergine, preferably over a gas hob on a low heat, until blackened all over. Alternatively roast the aubergine in a hot oven (220°C/gas mark 7) for 20–25 minutes. Carefully peel the aubergine and mash the creamy innards.

Cook the macaroni according to the pack instructions. Drain and transfer to a 25 x 20cm greased baking dish, reserving a little of the cooking water.

Meanwhile, melt the butter in a medium pan and stir in the flour. Cook the roux over a medium heat for 5 minutes, stirring constantly then gradually add the milk, stirring constantly.

Stir in the mustard, nutmeg, paprika, salt, pepper and cheese and stir until melted.

Stir in the smoked aubergine, cream and garlic, along with the reserved cooking water. Pour the sauce over the macaroni and mix well. Sprinkle generously with the extra grated cheese.

Bake at 180°C/gas mark 4 for 20–25 minutes until golden brown.

'SUVICHE' (sushi made with ceviche)

The cuisines of Mexico and Japan meet and enjoy the most civil of partnerships in this light, citrusy twist on the maki roll. You'll need the freshest sashimi-grade fish you can lay your hand on, so fresh that you can safely eat it raw, but a little goes a long way.

Serves 4

For the fish and marinade
200g sashimi-grade fish, eg 100g salmon and 100g mackerel, skinned and pin boned
1 teaspoon salt
juice of ½ lime
½ red onion, finely sliced
1 tablespoon soy sauce
1 tablespoon rice vinegar
1 red chilli, finely chopped

Lay the fish in a non-metallic shallow dish. Sprinkle with salt, lime juice, the red onion slices, soy sauce, rice vinegar and chilli. Cover and leave in the fridge for a couple of hours to 'cook'.

For the rice
200g sushi rice (preferably brown)
1 piece dried seaweed, eg wakame or kombu
2 teaspoons soy sauce
4 tablespoons rice vinegar
2 tablespoons caster sugar

To prepare the sushi rice wash it in a sieve. Leave it in the sieve to absorb any excess water for 30 minutes.

Place the rice in a heavy-based, lidded saucepan and add 220ml cold water. Place a piece of dried seaweed in there and pop the lid on. Heat over a medium heat until you hear it puttering and boiling away. Boil for 5 minutes, then turn the heat off to allow it to steam for a further 10 minutes. Mix the soy sauce, rice vinegar and sugar together and fold carefully into the cooling rice. Fan the rice to help it cool down quickly, making it more gelatinous with a nice glossy finish.

For the guacabi
2 avocados
1 clove garlic, crushed
2-3 teaspoons wasabi paste
few drops of hot pepper sauce
juice of ½ lime

Peel and mash the avocadoes with the garlic, wasabi, hot pepper sauce, lime juice and a pinch of salt. Cover and chill in the fridge.

To serve
4–6 sheets nori
½ medium cucumber, cut into strips

Place the nori sheet (glossy side down) on a bamboo sushi mat. Spread out a square of rice over this leaving a big seam at the top to allow room to fold in on itself. Spread the fish along the bottom of the rice in a straight line. Smear over a fat blob of guacabi and some cucumber strips. Roll up. Repeat to use up all the fish, rice and nori. Ideally, eat immediately while the rice is still warm, but it can be prepared in advance and chilled for a couple of hours.

ARTICHOKE CANNELLONI
with chilli, garlic & lemon

For those fateful times when you've fallen out big time with your poor, overworked liver and want to say sorry in the most savoury manner possible. Those deli counter tubs of marinated artichokes are handy for more than just lobbing into salads or mezze platters. By combining with health-endowing superheroes like chilli, garlic and lemon, you'll be duly forgiven and fighting fit in next to no time.

Serves 4-6

For the tomato sauce
1 tablespoon olive oil
1 garlic clove, crushed
2 tablespoons red wine
400g can chopped tomatoes
1 tablespoon chopped fresh sage
pinch of salt
pinch of sugar

Heat the olive oil in a small pan. Add the garlic, wine, tomatoes, sage, pinch of salt and sugar and simmer over a low heat for 15-20 minutes. You want a well flavoured sauce which isn't too dry and still has plenty of juice.

For the artichoke sauce
175g marinated artichoke hearts, oil
    reserved and finely chopped
2 garlic cloves, finely chopped
1 dried red chilli
300g spinach
2 tablespoons pine nuts
100g ricotta cheese
juice of ½ lemon
60g Parmesan cheese, grated
12 cannelloni tubes
1 teaspoon salt
125g mozzarella cheese, sliced

Preheat the oven to 200°C/gas mark 6.

In another small pan, drizzle in a little of the reserved artichoke oil and gently fry the garlic and chilli for 5 minutes. Add the artichokes and stir in the spinach until just wilted. Cool.

Toast the pine nuts in a hot, non-stick, dry frying pan until fragrant. Chop the spinach mixture and transfer to a large mixing bowl. Add the toasted pine nuts, ricotta, lemon juice, Parmesan and salt to the spinach mixture and stir well.

Using a teaspoon, stuff the mixture into the cannelloni tubes. Spread a layer of cannelloni tubes on the bottom of a baking dish. Cover in the tomato and sage sauce. Top with the mozzarella and bake for 40 minutes.

VANILLA CHURROS

with cardamom-coconut chocolate sauce

Full fat cola, greasy junk food, salty snacks – there's a very good reason why you might crave these no no's when you're body's running low on power. These are the times when that salad and smoothie just aren't going to cut it. Sometimes you just have to admit defeat and concede that only a Spanish doughnut dipped in softly spiced chocolate is going to sort you out.

Makes 20

For the chocolate sauce
6 cardamom pods
90g caster sugar

100g milk chocolate, roughly broken
100g dark chocolate, rougly broken
150ml coconut milk

Split the cardamom pods (reserving the husks) and grind the seeds using a pestle and mortar. Stir the seeds into the sugar and set aside to infuse for as long as you can (it's quite nice to keep a jar of this in the cupboard for stirring into tea).

Gently heat the chocolate, coconut milk and reserved cardamom husks in a small pan. Remove from the heat until you are ready to serve.

For the churros
125g plain flour
125g self-raising flour
2 tablespoons olive oil

pinch of salt
1 teaspoon vanilla extract
sunflower or groundnut oil, for deep frying

Mix the flours together and make a well in the centre. In a jug, mix the olive oil, salt and 450ml boiling water together. Pour this into the well and beat to whisk out any lumps. Stir in the vanilla extract. You should be left with a soft, sticky dough. Let this rest for 10 minutes.

In a large pan or deep fat fryer heat the oil to 170°C or until a cube of stale bread browns in 60 seconds.

Fit a piping bag with a 25mm star nozzle and spoon the dough into the bag. Squeeze fat lines of this straight into the hot oil, cook batches of 3-4 at a time, taking care not to overfill the pan. Fry for 3-4 minutes or until puffed and golden and drain well on kitchen paper. Sprinkle the churros with the cardamom sugar. Repeat to cook the remaining dough.

Remove the cardamom husks from the sauce, and serve the sauce in a bowl alongside the sugared churros for liberal dipping.

FROZEN CHERRY YOGURT KNICKERBOCKER GLORY

This satisfies the craving for sweet without the guilt-factor. It's like having all the virtue of a fruit salad with all the fun of a vintage British pud.

Serves 4

butter, for greasing

For the frozen cherry yogurt
200g cherry compote or jam
400ml Greek yogurt
150g cherries, stoned

Mix all the ingredients in an ice cream churner and freeze. Alternatively freeze the mixture and stir every 30 minutes until set.

For the roasted peaches and almond tuiles
2 ripe peaches, halved and stoned
1 teaspoon vanilla paste
2 tablespoons orange blossom or
    lavender honey
20g flaked almonds

100g butter
100g sugar
3 egg whites
50g plain flour
50g ground almonds

Preheat the oven to 200°C/gas mark 6. Place the peaches cut side up in a roasting tin. Mix the vanilla with the honey and drizzle this over. Roast the peaches for about 30 minutes, or until nicely caramelised. Reduce the oven temperature to 180°C/gas mark 4.

Line 2 baking trays with greased baking parchment. Toast the flaked almonds in a hot, non-stick, dry frying pan until fragrant. Cream together the butter and sugar. Slowly add the egg whites and gradually add the flour. Chill for 15 minutes. Drop teaspoonfuls of the almond tuile mixture onto the baking trays leaving room for them to spread. Bake for 3 minutes then sprinkle over the toasted flaked almonds. Return to the oven and cook for another 2-3 minutes, until golden. Leave to cool on the tray for a couple of minutes, and then put on a wire rack to cool completely.

To serve
170g raspberries
juice of ½ lime
1 banana

12 whole fresh cherries
75g almond chocolate, roughly broken
500g mixed strawberries, blueberries and
    blackberries

To make the coulis, whizz the raspberries, lime juice and banana in a blender. Melt the chocolate over a pan of gently simmering water. Holding a cherry carefully by its stalk, dip it into the melted chocolate, place on baking parchment to set.

Spoon some of the raspberry-banana coulis in the bottom 4 sundae glasses. Top this with the mixed fruit. Roughly crush in three almond tuiles. Add a scoop or two of the frozen cherry yogurt. Top with a roasted peach half and drizzle over some of the caramelised honey juice. Finally, add another tuile biscuit, some more frozen yogurt, the remaining coulis and top each with 3 chocolate almond cherries.

FIVE-A-DAY CAKE

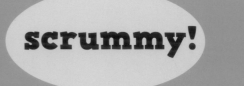

scrummy!

Moist, luscious and benevolent to your tastebuds as well as transporting you a fair distance towards your daily vit fix, a fat slice of this plus a hot mug of tea really will make everything better. It may seem a bit 'wet' at first, so is best eaten after a few hours, when all the juices have been absorbed. Kind of like a cross between an upside down cake and a carrot cake, this is a real analgesic to stress, ill health or general down in the dumpsitis. Think of it as the taste equivalent of a soothing hand on your poor, fevered brow softly whispering 'there, there, there' with every mouthful.

Serves 6-8

For the topping
120g butter plus extra for greasing
120g muscovado sugar
300g mixed apricots, peaches plums and greengages, sliced

Preheat the oven to 180°C/gas mark 4. Grease and line 2 x 20cm springform cake tins with baking parchment.

Heat the butter and sugar together in a small pan and pour it into one of the prepared tins. Place concentric circles of the apricot, peach, plum or greengage slices over the butter mixture.

For the cake
250g self-raising wholemeal flour
2 teaspoons baking powder
1 teaspoon ground cinnamon
1 teaspoon ground ginger
250g demerara sugar
150g parsnip, grated
100g carrot, grated
50g walnuts or pecans, roughly chopped
1 medium eating apple, grated
180ml olive oil
3 large eggs
100ml clear blossom or lavender honey
zest and juice of 1 clementine or satsuma

In a large bowl, mix the flour, baking powder, cinnamon, ginger, sugar, parsnip, carrot, nuts and apple. Add the olive oil, eggs, honey and citrus zest and juice mixing everything well.

Pour evenly into the prepared tins and bake for about 50 minutes or until an inserted skewer comes out clean. Leave the cakes in the tins to cool for a few minutes, then turn out onto a wire rack.

For the filling
1 large banana
200g cream cheese
450g icing sugar
dash of rum
100g unsalted butter

Mash the banana in a medium bowl, stir in the cream cheese, icing sugar, rum and butter, mix well and chill. Spread the filling over the cooled, plain cake. Place the fruit topped sponge on the filling topped sponge and sandwich them carefully together.

INDEX

delish!

ACKNOWLEDGEMENTS

Huge thanks to all at Kyle Books, in particular Emma Bastow and Judith Hannam. A special thank you to Rosemary Scoular for all the advice and for being generally amazing and also the wonderful Wendy Millyard. Also thanks to Chris Terry for the awesome photos, Anna Jones for the styling, and Nicky Collings for the brilliant design. And finally of course thanks to Joe and Ivan for the endless recipe testing, patience, mountains of washing up and love. I couldn't have done it without you.